February 9 1934

To Jones Hinckle
Eagel

Dear frend wolcott your letter receved
monday & was very glad to here from you
and to here you are well But very sorrow
and suprised to here of your mother death
i sure will mice her she has bin a very
good frend to me well wolcott this sure
is a tuff winter here the Bay is frozen
up our Boats frozen in the harbor we
can walk to little spruse and to
nork island down huckleBerrie head
and crab tree point worth more
i am aging those few lines but dont no
when i will get to the post ofice wether
of sel cold stern thur 12 Belo zero this morning
is not up ice last weak had 20 inch thick
thie is nothing we cando now But just look
aften our Boats and craft woot for stoves
wolcott and i was over to spruce head and
helped to post the ice up over there 2 weeks
ago only had 12 inches we are agoing to
post up another cuttting next weak
we pa all well at island that wether
to be thankful for this offel winter wolcott
goes gunning once and a vide to pass time away
he got 2 misslers yestday and he got 2
to day we ar agoing to have them backed
for dinner sunday dear frend Jesse
getta fetw lines more this feB 11 havent
got to post ofice yet and dont no how
long it will be before i get there there
is too much ice it isent dafe to walk and
cant get a boat out well woloott i was
over to great spruce head to day pitting
the sescked cutten of ice and dead
howard pote the mail there to us to day
so i receved your litter of feBuary 5
and check for fenuary and thanks
you very much for the extenopen anyting

your mother hant payed me up
for December I i will inclose the last
letter i received from her so as there
will be no miss under standing well
nelsott the ice braker Boat mane de
kickabus is having quit a job Braking
ice in penoscott bay this winter she
is coming to eagel island tomorow with
some supplies she has bin to north haven
and stonoton and to swans island
and she is clering the wester chanel
open between isbsly and little spruce
for the big tramp steamers to get
there to stocton spings corner
nither or ell dont no of eny thing now
for present time so will coll to a close
for now
                February 16 still ice
bound but. Bony gwin got to ploe
bed last night and is going to eagle
today and i an agoing to try and give
him this litter to mely so will close
        Best regards from
all to all
        Yours Handie
        eagel
        maine

Island Man

The Life and Letters of
Jim Hardie

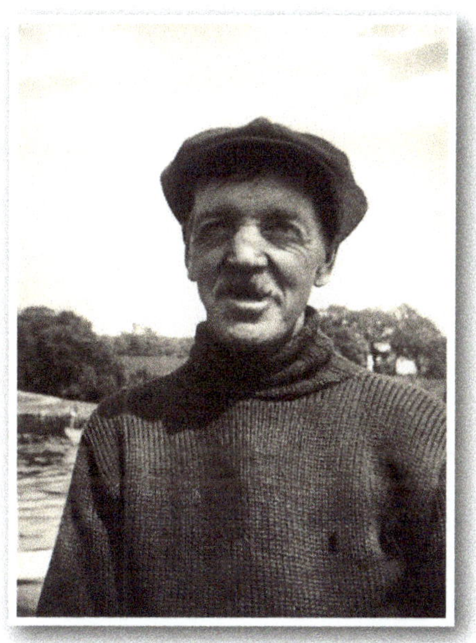

Lucilla Fuller Marvel

Island Man: The Life and Letters of Jim Hardie
2022 © Lucilla Fuller Marvel
ISBN 979-8-9858759-1-1

Publishing consulting, cover, and book design: Lindy Gifford, ManifestIdentity.com
The photographs from the Bear Island Family Archives, many of which are from albums assembled by Rosamond Fuller Kenison, are so identified and used with permission. The photographs of Geoffrey Baker are so identified and used with permission. All other images are used with permission.

On the cover: Jim at the wheel of his boat, 1940. (Geoffrey Baker photo)

Contents

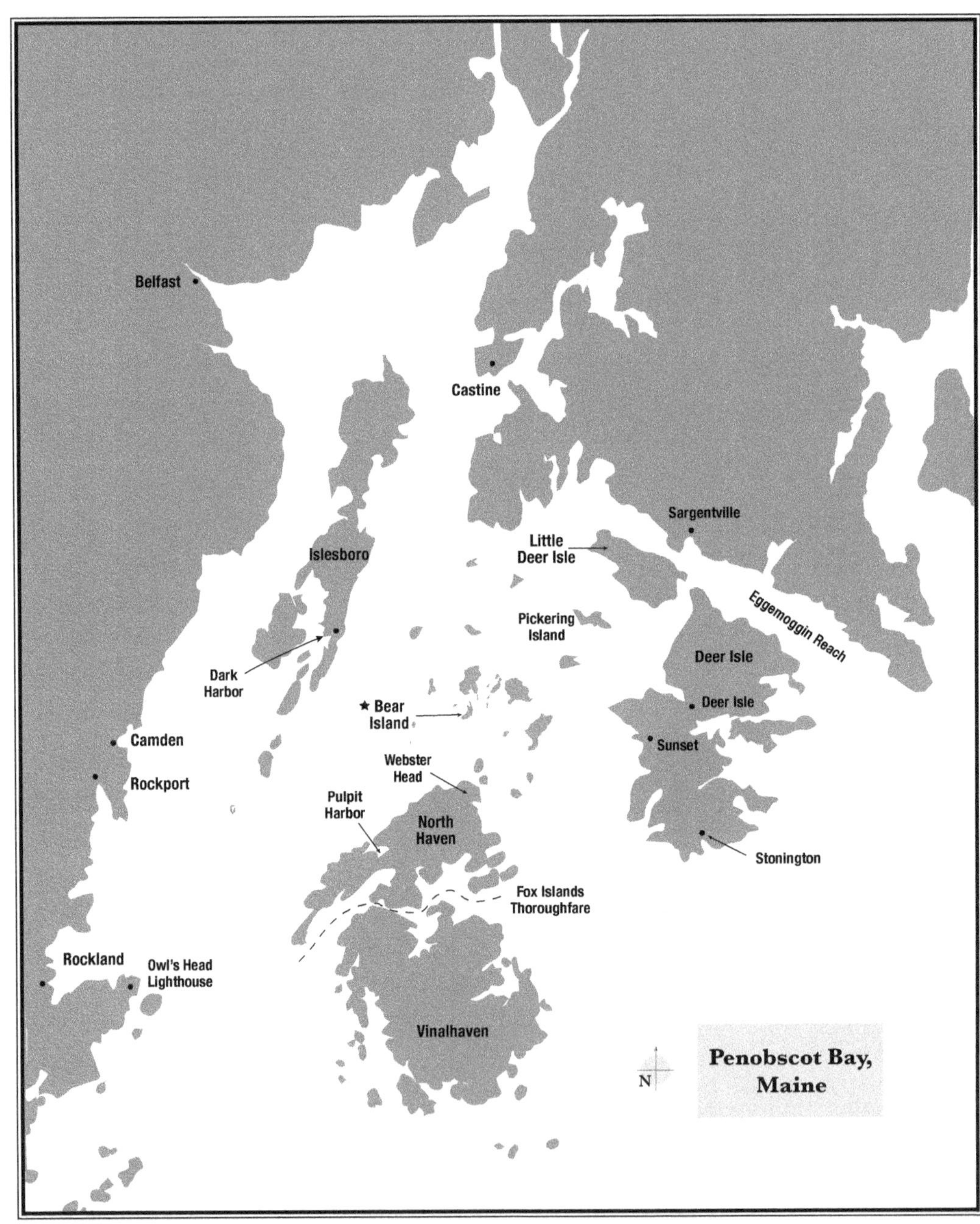

MAP DRAWN BY ISABEL JANE MARVEL

Foreword

Jim Hardie—An Archetype of a Maine Island Man

In 1904, the same year that Caroline Wolcott Andrews bought Bear Island in northern Penobscot Bay, the eminent president of Harvard, Charles Eliot, published an admiring biography of an American archetype: *John Gilley: Maine Farmer and Fisherman*. Gilley was an accomplished fisherman and farmer on Sutton Island, at the entrance to Northeast Harbor on Mount Desert Island, where Eliot was an early "rusticator." If Eliot had rusticated in Penobscot Bay, he might well have written an equally admiring monograph titled *Jim Hardie of Bear Island: Maine Farmer and Fisherman*. Thankfully, Caroline Andrews' great-granddaughter Lucilla Fuller Marvel has taken up Eliot's mantle.

To all who knew him, Jim Hardie was a phenomenal individual. Tall, lean, and muscular, he cut a striking figure. He was almost supernaturally capable. Captain, fisherman, farmer, hunter, boat builder, carpenter—these were only some of his many talents. But perhaps Hardie's most important attribute is what Caroline's grandson, the multitalented Buckminster Fuller, recalled as

Hardie's "gargantuan will." Island life attracts strong characters, and strong characters are attracted by island life. Jim Hardie's life is a testament to this observation.

In retrospect, perhaps it's not surprising that the force of Hardie's iron will would be singled out. Hardie was orphaned and at an early age shipped from Scotland to Prince Edward Island, Canada, to work long hours on a potato farm. After years of unpaid labor, however, Hardie ran away to sea. He was just twelve years old. Hardie shipped out first as a cabin boy and later as an able-bodied seaman and hunter aboard brutally harsh British sealing voyages to the Antarctic.

After a decade at sea, Hardie had acquired enough savings to leave the second ordeal of his life behind. No one knows how Hardie found his way to Little Deer Isle on the eastern shores of Penobscot Bay, but he soon found work with Lewis Shepard on nearby Pickering Island. Within a year Hardie had married Shepard's daughter, Alice. The two of them would remain islanders in Penobscot Bay for the next forty-four years, until he collapsed from a heart attack while cutting up alders on nearby Scrag Island. It's no surprise that Hardie was attracted to island life—the smaller the island, the better he liked it—because on islands all of his talents and experiences were especially valued. As caretaker—really, more of a "Captain"—on Bear Island for thirty-six years, he made island life possible for the summer folk.

Of Hardie's many extraordinary capabilities and feats, however, none are as remarkable as his success in teaching himself to read and write. As Marvel's captivating biography here recounts, Hardie would listen to the news on the radio and then study the captions under the pictures in a newspaper account of the same news story he had heard. He learned to associate the sounds of names he recalled with their spelling in newspapers and slowly gained his own phonetic fluency with the written language. To a willful individual who had taught himself everything he needed to know in order to survive—and ultimately thrive—acquiring the difficult and mysterious ability to communicate with the extended Fuller clan through laboriously crafted letters is truly remarkable.

Thankfully, Lucilla Fuller Marvel has assembled Jim Hardie's letters and life in this lively volume, which is more than just a compelling chronicle of island life. It is the story of the triumph of a Maine island man and his family.

Philip Conkling
Lanes Island, Vinalhaven

Sunday June 21 1914

Dear frend wilket i have received your letter today and am axcenn rite away in regord to the island i rote to your Mother a weak and a haelf ago and told her all about things now about the tennes cort is in good order and i have a nice vegtable garden and we have the cook house clended and the big house they are all in good order now about a Boat the rite Bear is not fuclhed yet But my Boats is in good order and your mother can hare her on the scame terms as last year so thet is oll for this time we are oll well and

from James Hardie
lageli po
Bear island
Maine

**Letter from Jim Hardie to Wolcott Fuller, June 21, 1914,
the first in his collection of forty-one letters**

Preface

About the Letters and the Evolution of This Book

In 1904, my great-grandmother, Caroline Matilde Wolcott Andrews, bought an island in the middle of Penobscot Bay in Maine. It was her gift to her grandchildren and future heirs for a place to spend their summers. Islands and properties needed someone to look after them. In 1910, James Hardie was hired to be the year-round caretaker and live on Bear Island.

Life on Bear Island—or Bear as it is also called—was to transform generations of lives of those who stayed there, and continues to do so. Many are the beneficiaries of its beauty, family ties, and friendships. However, this work is not a history of Bear Island and its summer family. The island still remains in the hands of some of Caroline Wolcott Andrews's descendants today. That is another story.

This book records and celebrates the life of one man, James Hardie—Jim—whose legacy remains; his strength of character, capability for survival through nature's four seasons, and willingness to work with the family of owners. Jim's presence, then, makes our presence today possible.

Jim's letters are the basis of this book. Most of the letters were written to my father, Wolcott Fuller, who was one of Caroline Andrews's grandsons. I found them in a box of my father's papers after his death in 1959, kept in a file entitled "Letters of Capt. James Hardie, Bear Island, Maine." The bulk of these letters date from 1914 until 1937, and then there are a few more until 1954, when Jim died.

The letters are a rich treasure trove of an extraordinarily resourceful man. Born in 1884 in Scotland, Jim was sent to Canada as an orphan. At a young age, he ran away from his foster home on Prince Edward Island in the Maritime provinces, shipped out on sealing vessels to Antarctica, made his way into the United States in 1907, and spent the rest of his life on islands in Penobscot Bay, Maine.

Jim's letters tell firsthand the experiences that he and his large family went through and endured as the only year-round residents of Bear Island. For three of the seasons, and especially during the harsh wintertime, they were the single family on Bear's forty-two acres. Most of the letters were written when the owners and their families were not on the island for their summer vacations. From his letters we learn that Jim was self-reliant, with an innate intelligence and ability to carry out the wide range of tasks required of a full-time caretaker and provider for his own family through fishing and farming. Jim relates the challenges that he and his family survived of living with the seasons, living with hard times.

The letters are remarkable in another way. As lively and descriptive as they are, they are written in a language he developed. What little schooling he had had on Prince Edward Island was behind him when he went to sea at age twelve. Sometime before settling in Maine, he taught himself to read and write in his own fashion.

According to Buckminster Fuller (Bucky, my father's brother), Jim used words he heard on the radio, combined with words he saw under pictures in newspapers, to make sense out of language. "Thus, he taught himself to read and write—a truly great feat," Bucky wrote in 1967 in an unpublished manuscript titled "The Bear Island Story."[1] Jim's letters are evidence of his phonetic spelling, writing, and verbal skills with which he expressed his thoughts and observations well. Jim seldom used punctuation and generally separated his thoughts by spacing. He consistently capitalized only a few letters of the alphabet, such as *J*, *H*, and *B*. One assumes that he learned to capitalize the initials of his name and perhaps that of the name of his foster family on Prince Edward Island.

Many of the letters in the Wolcott Fuller collection are included in excerpts in this book. Most are addressed to Wolcott, with a few addressed jointly to Caroline Andrews Fuller, his mother, and to her sister, Lucy Andrews King. There are several letters from Alice Shepard Hardie, Jim's wife.

Realizing the letters to be such a valuable source of information about an independent life on an island in Maine, I wanted to make them accessible. The originals in Jim's handwriting are a challenge to read, so in the summer of 1975, I typed copies of the letters. The typed version is as close as possible to the way Jim put his words down on paper. Reading the letters out loud helps to understand the individual words. One example, *"i shood itfidse you,"* if written in grammar school English, would become "I should advise you." A careful reading shows that there was some Scottish and Canadian influence in the way he wrote, as the letter "a" is often written as "o." "All" is consistently spelled "oll," and "awful" is always "offel."

I then sent copies of the typed letters to members of the Bear Island family as well as to Jim's youngest son, Pearl Hardie, and his family. At that time, I thought that a reading of the letters stood by themselves in telling Jim's dramatic story of a man and an island.

It was only much later, in 2004, as we prepared to celebrate the centennial of summers on Bear Island by Andrews family descendants, that I started to write about Jim and the Hardie family too. They have been an integral part of the island history. This led me to do research about Jim. I looked for biographical material not included in the letters and gathered anecdotes from Jim's living relatives. I talked with his son Pearl and Pearl's wife, Evelyn, about my intention of writing about the Hardies. They were very pleased and willing to share information and anecdotes about Jim and his wife, Alice.

My first essay became a chapter, "The Hardie Family," in the *Bear Island Centennial Book 1904–2004*, published in 2009.[2] The *Island Journal*, the annual publication of the Island Institute in Rockland, Maine, in its 2012 edition included my article, "The Life and Letters of Jim Hardie: Fisherman, Farmer, Captain, Caretaker."[3] Both documents were illustrated with photographs. From our family albums came pictures taken in the first half of the twentieth century. A valuable part of the visual historical legacy is the photos taken by Geoffrey Baker in 1940. Mr. Baker, an architect, was a guest with his family on Bear Island at that time; he and his family subsequently acquired a summer home on another island in Penobscot Bay.

Since writing those pieces, I continued to inquire about Jim and reflect on his earlier life and gather material. I was fortunate to have access to other letters from Jim, saved by my father's sister, Rosamond ("Rosy") Fuller Kenison, and stored by her daughter, Kariska K. Puchalski, corresponding to the years 1938 until 1946, years my father's collection did not cover.

Official documents and data about Jim's life are few. His immigration and naturalization papers for US citizenship date from 1942 to 1943. Pearl Hardie's wife, Evelyn, gave me a copy in 2016. The papers reveal that Jim first attempted to file for citizenship at Ellsworth, Maine, on April 12, 1917. In 1942, during World War II, he filled out the full application to become a citizen of the United States: "Statement of Facts to be used in Making My Declaration of Intention." He states that his occupation is a fisherman; his place of residence is Bear Island, Maine; and that he was born in Scotland. Jim's response to other questions was "Do not know."

The letters are the main feature of this book, as nothing comes close to Jim's voice. On March 24, 1918, he wrote:

> *i tell you we have had a terrebel winter here you cood go eanny ware on the ice   there hase Bin some men walk from pulpit harBer to camden this winter   But i did not go much on the ice for i dont like it gong on the ice without i go to   But i did walk to eagel and to Derigo once But i walke to great sproos head about all winter   i had to go to sproos head eavry day i got in the ice one day gong over there and i found the water cind of cold i was all rite for i had a Boat with me holing her over the ice and wen i broke thrue i made a Jump in my Boat*

For this book, I have written short narratives or chapters organized around a chronology of Jim's life, his family, his interaction with the summer family, and the story lines that Jim covers in his letters, such as news of the bay and the weather. Excerpts from his letters are included throughout. As suggested earlier, reading them out loud gives meaning to Jim's words.

This work does not pretend to be a biography of Jim; however, with the material on hand it does intend to be a portrait of a remarkable man. In 1975, when I transcribed the letters, many of Jim's children and grandchildren were alive, and had I asked them, they could have provided so much more to the Jim Hardie story, relating to the years after he left Bear Island in 1946. At that time, he and his wife, Alice, moved to neighboring Scrag Island, where he died in 1954. If willing, they could have provided descriptions of how their own lives had evolved and how growing up on Bear had influenced their families and livelihood.

I knew from early on that Jim's life of sustained survival was a compelling tale, and so for nearly fifty years I've been motivated to piece together this remarkable story. It resonates deeply with today's global struggles for social justice: an orphaned immigrant, lacking formal education, making his hardscrabble way against all odds. It is Jim's voice, a voice equal to any, that I want to be heard and provoke thought.

Perhaps some of Jim's grandchildren and great-grandchildren will be inspired to gather more history and anecdotes to enrich and document the Hardie family history. I am grateful to those who have contributed their time and information for this work over the years, especially Evelyn Hardie.

January 28 / 1924

Janes Hardie
eagle ill

Dear frend wolcott i jos drop
you a few lines to let you no how we
are geting along well wolcet we are
all well at present and hoping you
are well and geting along all right
well wolcott i reced the thinges
you sent me allright and i thank
you verry much and also a long time
ago i received the glosses wich you
sent me and they are verry good
glosses to me and i thank you
verry much for then well wolcott
we have bin having some offel
good weather for the time of
year up until a weak ago But
since that we have had it offel
Bad the wind changes about every
day and it Blows a gel every
way it comes we are having a very
cold snap at present yestday
the tempther was 26 Blow sero

) 2 (

But this morning it is 18
Blow sero you no that is offel
cold fore here for the tempther
dont drop here like it dos on
the main the salt are dont let
it droop like it wood ware it
is dry cold yestday olday
the keper was thick like fog
that i cornot see the other end
of the island once and a wile
it wood shut the Boat house
in But it has made no salt water
ice yet to mount to eny thing yet
ofcorse it carnot freos very much
ice for it Blowes to hard it
wont let the water smooth enough
i was over to camden last monday
i left home i had farly good weak
thers was a little wind west when
i got over to Jo Bis island Bou the
western Bay was feather wite
and it was just sero when
ther and when i got into camden

Four-page letter from Jim Hardie to Wolcott Fuller, January 28, 1924—pages 1 and 2.

)3(

The genrel Knof was all shearded
over with ice the spray wood fly
over her and freas as fast as it
cane over her Belive me wolcott the
old genrel Knof will go to the
windred as long if as we can
loof to windad By the tine
i was redy for hone again
i it cane some show syoles fro
the west and Blowed a liven
gal well i started for hone
and Belive me there was sone
sea aBout that til i
cane from canden worf to
Bear island worf in 74 ninty
Josie and Janzey and Kinbel
and leuil was with me
and the Brakest man i had
was Janey But i tel you Josie
was very scored But the genrel
Knof run like a Bird on a wing
well wolcot i hope to sea you here
to the island next summer

)4(

and when you now your are
coming down for your your vackshe
let me no in tine and i will make
your Boat all rady for the water
and then you can youse her as
soon as you get here and then
you may get a chance to sell her
you no it is easer to sell a Boat
when she is in the water then
when she is on the Bank
they have no sal Boat to
spros head now for mister
porter sold the rose aBout
to mister shepard and mr
shepard striped her and
mad a power Boat of her
well wolcott i dont no of eny
thing more for this tine so
will close for this tine hoping
to here from you soon again
very trusy yours
Jim Hardie
eago mil

Four-page letter from Jim Hardie to Wolcott Fuller, January 28, 1924—continued, pages 3 and 4.

Jim's Early Life

Jim Hardie came from harsh beginnings. Not a lot is known about his early life, but it was a bleak one from the few facts available to piece together. Jim was born in Scotland in October 1884. This date for Jim's birth is engraved on his tombstone and is also in his obituary of 1954. According to the immigration and naturalization papers that Jim filled out in 1942–1943, he stated 1885 as the year of his birth. Although in later years Jim chose to celebrate his birthday on October 2, the actual date of his birth is not certain.[4] The stark reality of Jim's early life is revealed in the set of immigration and naturalization papers in which Jim replies "Do not know" to questions such as name of father, name of mother, and name of city or town of birth.

Jim was one of the thousands of youngsters shipped abroad from Great Britain, mainly from England, but also Scotland and Ireland, and sent principally to Canada as part of the "home children" movement. The Industrial Revolution of the nineteenth century caused rapid economic and population growth in British urban areas, benefitting many but also "creating a vast number of people who struggled simply to survive, living and working in unsafe and unsanitary conditions. In such cases a family broken by sudden death or economic circumstances had little by way of an extended family to fall back on."[5]

This condition led to vast numbers of pauper families, as they were called, who couldn't cope with their children, as well as children who were homeless, living in the streets. Books such as *The Little Immigrants: The Orphans Who Came to Canada*, by Kenneth Bagnell,[6] are filled with heartbreaking stories of abandoned children rescued from the streets of London, Birmingham, Liverpool, and Glasgow and placed in institutional homes and workhouses, where they were housed, fed, and given religious instruction and some schooling, depending on the age of the child. An ostensibly benevolent welfare plan emerged to help solve the problem of the growing number of children to care for and at the same time to help settle rural Canada by shipping over the Atlantic Ocean boatloads of young children and adolescents.

Upon landing, they were distributed to farming families who needed help on the farm or in the household. Agreements were signed: "known as Forms of Indenture [they were] intended not only to set out the farmers' responsibilities but to bind the children until they reached the age of eighteen."[7] The age of the children sent from Great Britain varied. "Most were in their teens, many were younger and a few were hardly out of their infancy."[8] There were different procedures for compensating the children for the work they performed. For the older children, it was simply room and board, with money set aside to be given to the child when he or she reached an age, often the age of 18, to become independent citizens. In some cases, the children received a small allowance on a monthly basis. In the majority of the cases, although schooling was promised, the children were not sent to school.

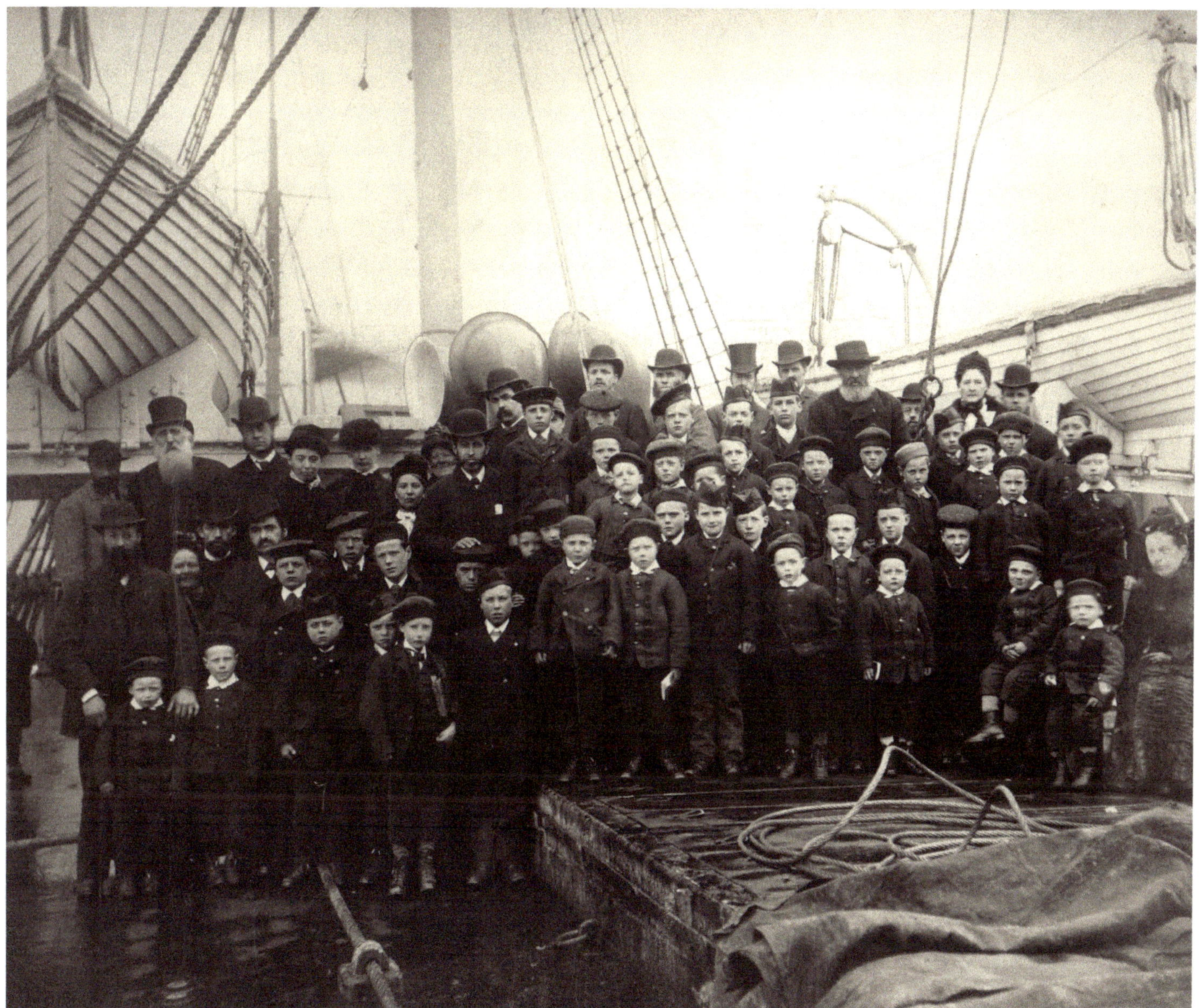

Orphan boys on board the SS *Norwegian* in 1885, en route from Scotland to Canada.
REPRODUCED WITH PERMISSION FROM QUARRIERS, SCOTLAND.

Between 1869 and the late 1930s, over 100,000 juvenile migrants were sent to Canada from Great Britain during the child emigration movement. Motivated by social and economic forces, churches and philanthropic organizations sent orphaned, abandoned and pauper children to Canada. Many believed that these children would have a better chance for a healthy, moral life in rural Canada, where families welcomed them as a source of cheap farm labour and domestic help.[9]

There was little supervision after the children were placed in their foster homes. Long working hours, sometimes even seven days a week, and physical punishment were often part of the upbringing, according to *The Little Immigrants*. The program of shipping children abroad met mounting criticism, and by the 1930s, child migration was disfavored and for the most part phased out. As Bagnell notes:

> If, as psychiatry has told us, the years of our childhood are the years that shape our inner lives forever, then the practice of child migration—the act of uprooting children and sending them, alone, across the ocean to work in a strange land in a strange occupation—must be regarded as one of the most Draconian measures in the entire history of children of English-speaking society. Its impact on the life of a sensitive child—even one who was placed in reasonable circumstances—is difficult to measure, sometimes difficult even to imagine.[10]

Thus at a tender age, Jim was shipped from Scotland to Nova Scotia in the Maritime provinces of Canada and then placed in a foster home on nearby Prince Edward Island. Jim could have been at least six or seven years old, old enough to work on a farm. "Approximately 150 home children were placed with families on Prince Edward Island,"[11] which to this day has a large Scottish population. It is estimated that more than a third (38–50 percent) of the residents have Scottish roots.

According to Jim's family, he was placed with a "Bowers" or "Bowser" family. Tracking down the placement of the "home children" is difficult in many cases because record keeping was not rigorous, and children were sometime switched from one family to another.

> On Prince Edward Island these arrangements were usually informal. Only rarely did the authorities in charge of child welfare coordinate such activity . . . sometimes to the despair of descendants trying to puzzle out their relationship in the family tree without any sort of paper trail to leave a clue.[12]

Nothing is known about his foster home, neither the family members nor the conditions of living. But they must have been miserable enough for him to determine to leave. According to his family, Jim ran away from the foster home at the age of twelve years. Buckminster Fuller, in the "The Bear Island Story," hints at the reasons: "At eight [*sic*] years of age he was convinced that he was being kept at home as a slave worker by his foster parents. He ran away to sea." Jim would leave Prince Edward Island with life lessons well learned. He had absorbed a knowledge of farming potatoes, then as now the principal agricultural crop of the island. And he would leave with a sense of how to live on an island.

An eight-mile channel separated Prince Edward Island from New Brunswick and Nova Scotia; the population was traditionally dedicated to an independent and self-sufficient way of life. As the bridge joining Prince Edward Island to New Brunswick was not built until 1997, Jim would have made his way by water to Saint John in New Brunswick, on the Bay of Fundy, which remains to this day an active sailing and fishing port.

Yet, however rough the Prince Edward Island experience was, Jim must have retained some desire to connect with his past and the foster family. According to Evelyn Hardie, he took his wife, Alice, and his sister-in-law, Josie Shepard, on a trip to visit Prince Edward Island and the family after World War II.[13]

After Jim had abandoned his foster home, he took to the sea. According to Buckminster Fuller:

> During the next 13 [*sic*] years he sailed first as a cabin boy and then as an able seaman in Antarctica sealing vessels. It was a tough life. His eyes became permanently bloodshot by exposure to the Antarctic Sun.

Sealing, or hunting seals and elephant seals for their pelts and oil, was notoriously difficult and punishing. Voyages on the sealing vessels, in Jim's day, usually in small schooners or barques, were demanding, often involving difficult weather conditions. The ships would drop off groups of sealers, called sealing gangs, on prospective hunting grounds. They could be left for months or longer, until the ships returned to pick up the men, the seal skins, and oil. William Dane Phelps in his memoirs describes being stranded for close to two years with seven other men, until they were picked up. The sealing gangs would have to fashion their own primitive form of shelter, often using the protection of caves and rocks, and survived on the bird and animal life available for food. Sealing was a bloody and brutal trade, as was the weather in Antarctica.[14]

At some point, when he was about twenty-one, Jim had saved enough wages to come ashore at Saint John, New Brunswick, and make his way to Maine. Information provided by Jim on his immigration and naturalization papers indicates that he arrived by train in Vanceboro, Maine, from "St. Johns [*sic*], N.B" on March 16,

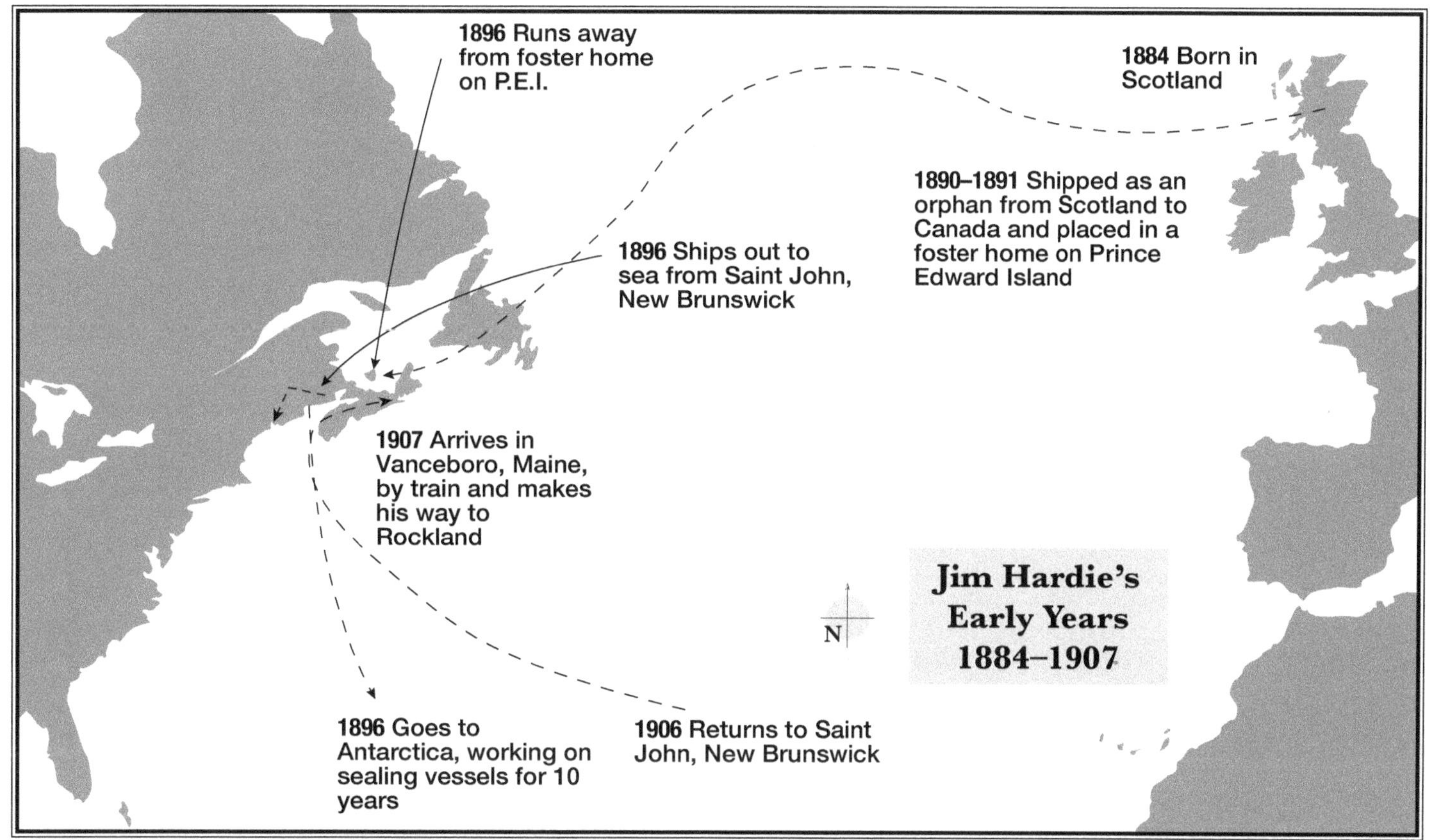

MAP DRAWN BY ISABEL JANE MARVEL

1907, headed for Rockland, Maine. Vanceboro, Maine, is across the St. Croix River from St. Croix, New Brunswick, and it was selected as the site for the crossing of the railway between Bangor, Maine, and Saint John, New Brunswick, in the 1860s.

The family believes that Jim worked in the Bath Iron Works before coming up into the East Penobscot Bay area. There, he landed on Little Deer Isle and decided to settle. Jim was employed in Sargentville on the mainland, possibly in the ice works, and also on Pickering Island with Lewis Shepard. Interestingly enough, Lewis was from Nova Scotia.[15] One wonders if the Maritimes connection brought them together. On April 25, 1909, Jim became part of the Shepard family when he married Alice Shepard, Lewis's daughter.

While seeking work on the islands, Jim first arrived on Bear Island in 1908. He rowed the six miles from Little Deer Isle in his "double-ended lapstrake, sailing/rowing pea-pod."[16] Peapods are small double-ended rowing and sailing boats used for near shore lobstering. Fisherman, standing up and facing forward, used them for rowing. He became the full-time caretaker on Bear Island for Mrs. Andrews and her family in 1910, taking the place of John Johnson, a minister, who had resigned to return to his preaching at Lincolnville, Maine.

Captain James Hardie was twenty-six years of age when he took up full-time residence on Bear Island with his wife, Alice, and their three-month-old daughter, Lillian. With his new job came the title—Captain—that he would have for the rest of his life. This tradition denoted respect for his position and knowledge of the sea. It also recognized a geographical hybrid, life on water-bound land. As Buckminster Fuller wrote, "Small islands then had Captains because . . . the sea concepts were felt to hold valid amongst the islands. Islands were unsinkable ships."[17]

By this time, Jim had shown the strength and resiliency to survive many hardships. He was up to the task. Orphaned, he was sent from his birthplace, across the Atlantic, to a foreign land. Living in a foster home in disagreeable, seemingly servant-like conditions, he made his first decision in independent living: to run away and be on his own. He had endured the grueling experience of working at sea on Antarctic sealing vessels. He had learned from his life's outset how to survive and take care of himself.

All that prepared Jim to take on the next thirty-six years of his life on Bear Island until 1946. On Bear he raised and took care of a large family, along with his wife, Alice; scraped together a meager living from fishing and caretaking; and rode out two world wars and the Great Depression. Jim mastered many skills, including boat building, house building, carpentry, navigation, fishing, and farming. He educated himself to read and write. A self-made man, he learned to get along with his employers and their families, whose daily lives and background were a stark contrast to his. The descendants of Mrs. Andrews and the Hardie family represented two worlds sharing one island. Jim's innate intelligence, resilience, and strength guided him through those two worlds.

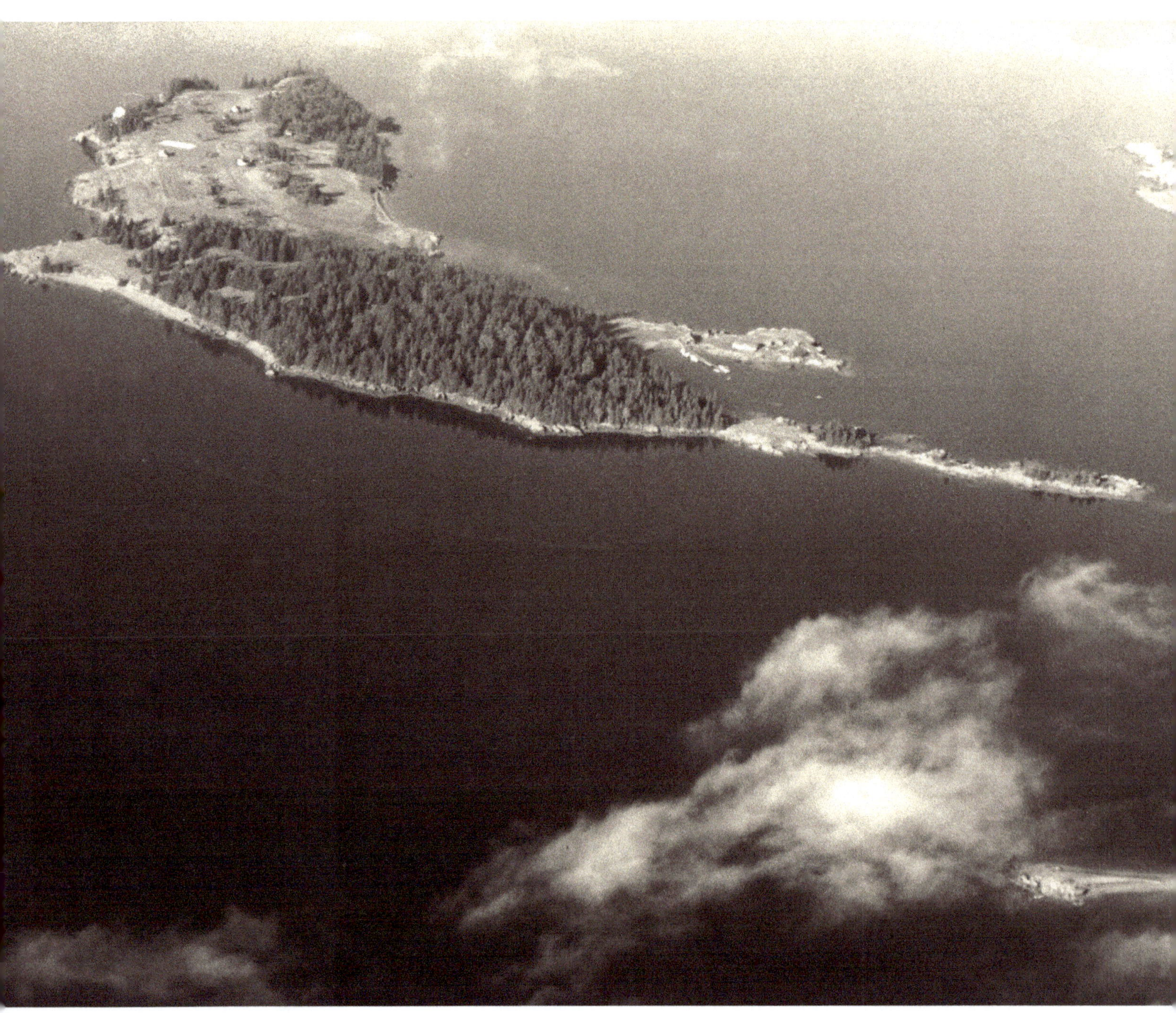

Aerial view of Bear Island, looking south, showing the Harbor in the middle and Scrag Island off to the west, 1940.
GEOFFREY BAKER PHOTO

Bear Island

At the turn of the twentieth century in the United States, opportunities and accommodations were plentiful for families who could afford to travel and take summer vacations. Caroline Matilde Wolcott Andrews lived in Chicago, and she was accustomed to travel "back East" in the summers.

Mrs. Andrews could board the popular overnight train in Chicago. Like many other passengers, within a day or so she could arrive at a relative's home, a vacation home, or check into a resort hotel. She was the widow of Martin Andrews and was seventy-four years old when she bought Bear Island in 1904. That year she had traveled with her oldest daughter, Lucy Andrews King, and her family, who also lived in Chicago. They planned to spend the summer in Milton, a suburb of Boston, with her youngest daughter, Caroline Andrews Fuller, and her family. However, an epidemic made them change their minds.

A 1971 letter from Rosy Fuller Kenison about the history of Bear Island explains, "The summer of 1904 there had been some kind of flu epidemic. . . . The family decided that all their children would be safer from contagion further away so they decided to try

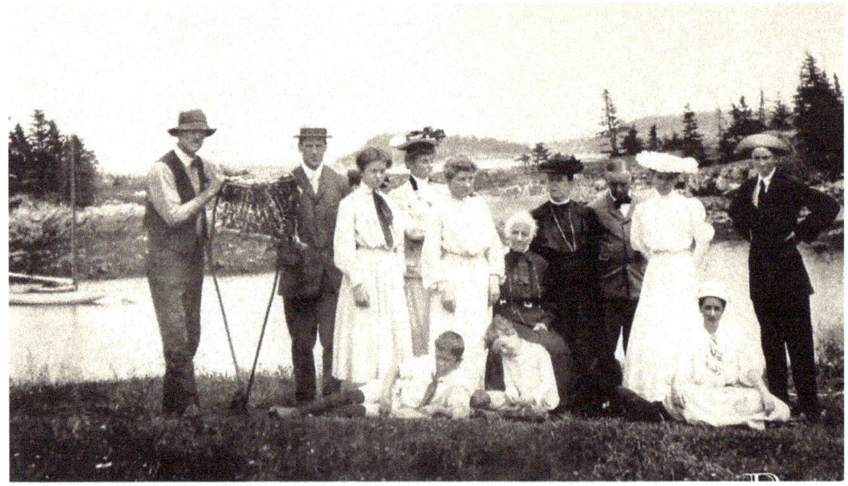

Jim, standing on the far left, and Grandmother Andrews, seated in center with her children and grandchildren, 1909.
BEAR ISLAND FAMILY ARCHIVES

Maine instead."[18] Mrs. Andrews and her family chose to vacation in Maine's Penobscot Bay. They stayed at a hotel on Eagle Island. While out boating, she spotted neighboring Bear Island and fell in love with it. In December of 1904, she purchased the island from the Eaton and Parsons families, who lived on the island during the last half of the nineteenth century. Bear Island, with its beautiful scenery, undisturbed nature, and pure air, seemed to Mrs. Andrews to be the perfect place to gather her children and grandchildren for summer vacations. She envisioned this as a family legacy. When she died in 1910, she left the island to her eight grandchildren, one of whom was my father.

Mrs. Andrews followed the path of many families to Maine: enamored of its untrammeled scenery, they wanted to return. Having first come as visitors, many purchased land to build summer homes. By the 1880s, there were an estimated 100,000 people staying in the hotels built along the Maine coast, including the hotels on neighboring Butter Island (the Dirigo Resort at that time) and Eagle Island. They traveled to Maine by water on such lines as the Boston and Bangor Steamship Line. After an overnight trip from Boston, they landed in cities like Rockland, as in the case of the Andrews-King-Fuller group. Those going to the islands would transfer to smaller boats or packets for the remainder of the trip. The Andrews party of five adults and seven children traveled on the Eastern Steamship Line's *City of Rockland*. There they chartered a little steam packet, *Juliet*, for the trip to Eagle Island.

These were families who could afford the time and expense to escape from noisy, crowded, and polluted industrialized cities for extended vacations. They were able to purchase property, including entire islands; build second homes; and hire the help to care for these places. The summer people were known from early days as "rusticators," and their summer homes were called cottages, no matter what the size. Even today, the summer folk are often referred to as people "from away," as are long-time, year-round residents if they are not originally from Maine, although they may have lived there for decades.

Bear Island is situated in the middle of Penobscot Bay, in midcoast Maine. It is located in Hancock County, part of that county's "unorganized territory." Penobscot Bay is one of Maine's largest bays. From the Atlantic Ocean, it runs twenty-five miles from the southern approach to the north at Bucksport, where the Penobscot River continues on to Bangor. Bear Island is roughly ten miles from the town of Camden on the mainland to the west, and about five miles from Sunset and its Sylvester Cove to the east, and the town of Stonington, both on Deer Isle.

Penobscot Bay abounds in islands, some large, some small rock ledges. It was settled more than five thousand years ago by the Penobscots, one of the Indigenous tribes recognized in Maine and Canada; then by Europeans and traders migrating north from Massachusetts and south along the coast from the Maritime provinces. Maine was part of Massachusetts until it became a state in 1820. By the mid-nineteenth century, the French and American battles for sovereignty were over, and the American Revolutionary War had passed. The Bay was recognized for its rich fishing grounds, valuable lumber supply, and excellent harbors. Bear Island, by 1850, had several families living on it, many of them Eatons and some Parsons. However, by 1900, when visitors to Eagle Island and Butter Island were touring the Bay by boat, looking at islands to buy, there were no full-time residents of Bear according to the US census.

Bear was not always known as Bear. "The name of the island was shown as Bear or Bare, interchangeably, from its earliest appearance on charts and in deed records until early in this century [twentieth]."[19] The 1904 deed refers to "Bear Island, so-called (sometimes known as Bare Island)," and Bear is what seems to have stuck.

Bear Island, measuring about "forty-two acres more or less,"[20] abounds in natural features. It has a deep protected harbor, several springs, and a varied coastline of sand and gravel beaches and cliffs. At the time Mrs. Andrews bought the island, it was quite bare, as it had been well lumbered and farmed like so many Maine islands.

The previous owners, the Eaton and Parsons families, left a fenced-in graveyard with several gravestones. When Mrs. Andrews purchased Bear, the deed stipulated that the previous owners and heirs had the right to access, use, and maintain the graveyard, adorned by a beautiful stand of lilac bushes.

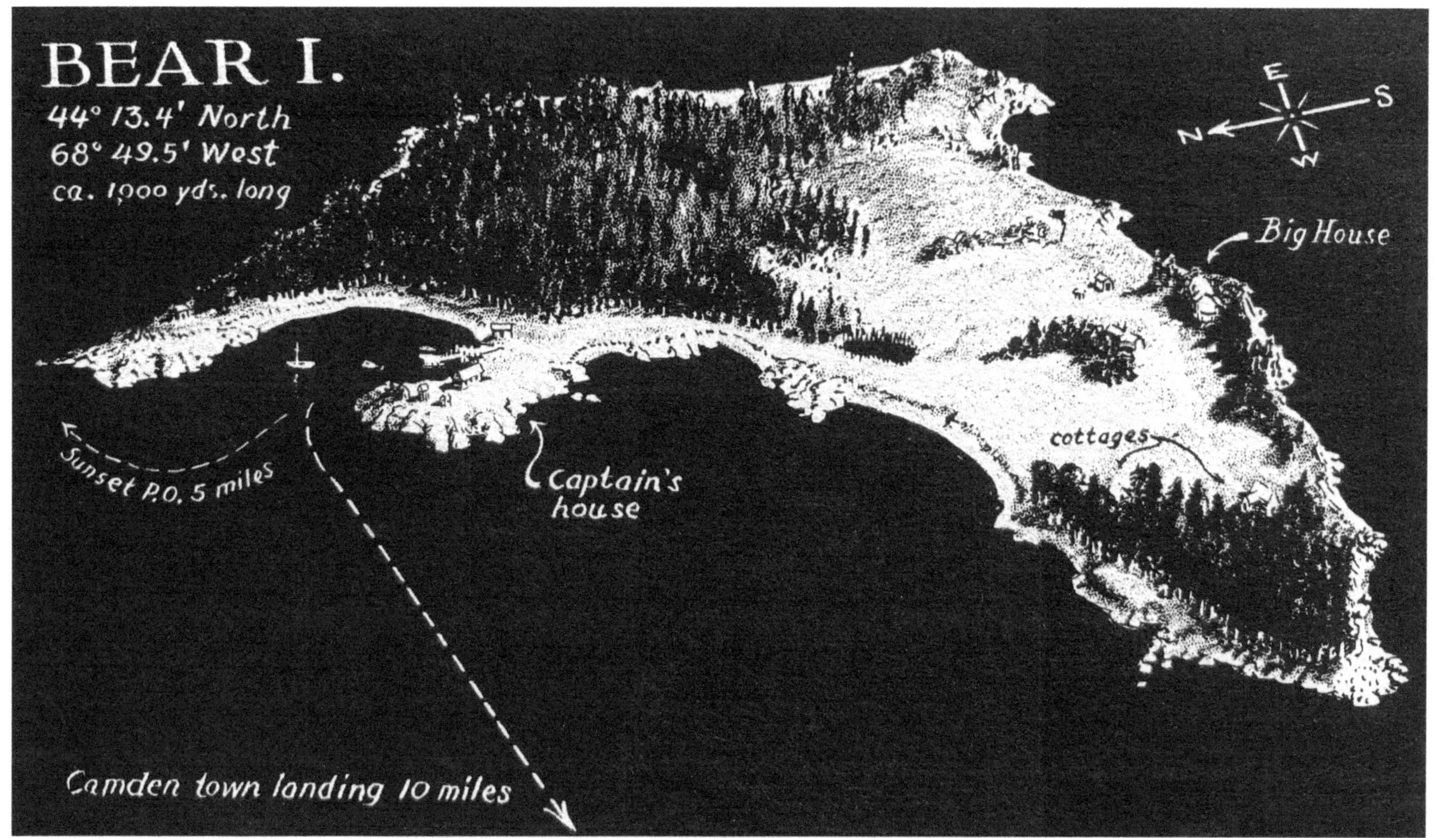

Bird's-eye view of Bear Island drawn by Richard Edes Harrison, 1941.   BEAR ISLAND FAMILY ARCHIVES

Several nineteenth-century farmhouses still stood in 1904. Two of these were fixed up and put to use as dwellings for the summer family, and another became the residence for the caretaker. They are still in use today. Over the past century, several more buildings and structures have been added. By choice, none of the buildings have indoor plumbing. Until fairly recently, kerosene lamps were the source for indoor lighting, today provided by solar power. Cook stoves were fueled by coal and wood, and now by propane. Today a diversity of fields and forests abound. The meadows and fields are home to an unfolding carpet of grasses and wildflowers. Hayfields continue to be mowed. Wildlife, both large and small, winged and four footed, is plentiful. Eagles have returned to soar above, battling with the osprey over nesting areas. The forested areas are a mixture of spruce and hardwoods, including oak, maple, and birch. Walking trails cover the island. If there is a crown jewel to be treasured and cared for among the hundreds of inhabited islands of the Coast of Maine, Caroline's heirs believe it is Bear. Those heirs, an amalgam of the fourth, fifth, sixth, and seventh generations, are dedicated to conserving and managing its natural beauty for the future. Such is the passion of those who love the Maine coast and are fortunate enough to be stewards of a part of it.

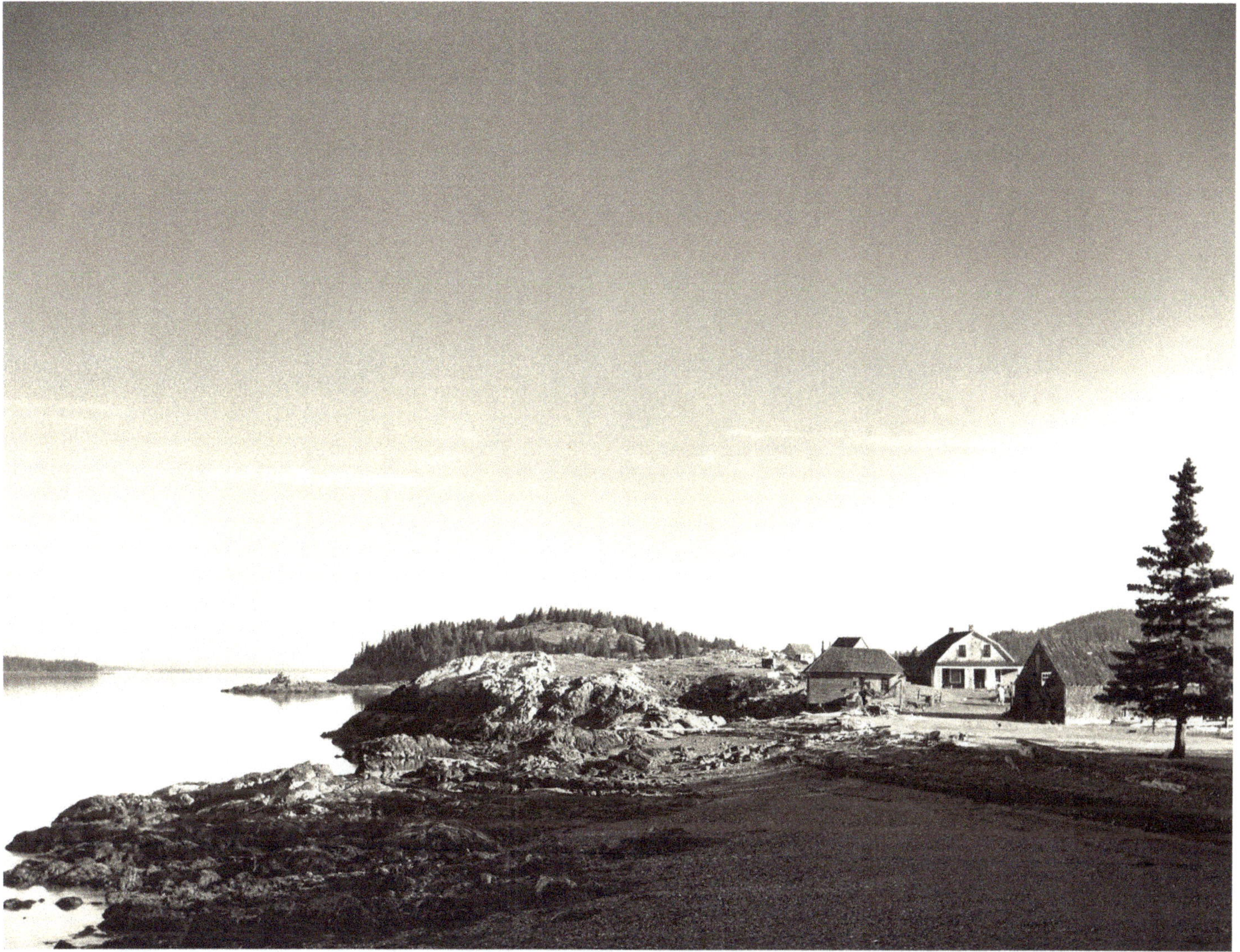

Approaching the Harbor area from the south; Great Spruce Head Island in the background, 1940.
GEOFFREY BAKER PHOTO

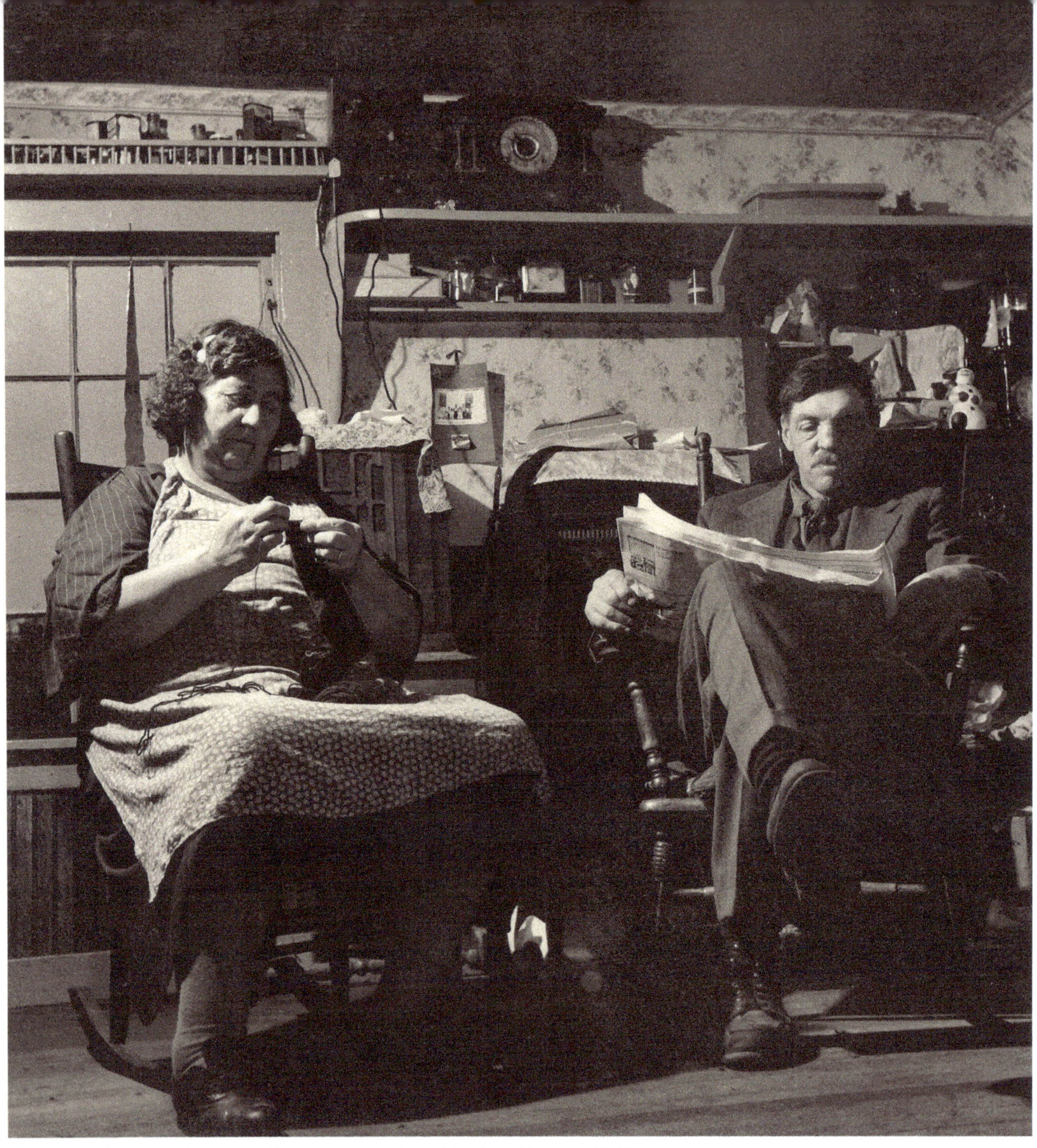

Alice and Jim Hardie in the living room of the Harbor House, 1940.   GEOFFREY BAKER PHOTO

Jim and Alice Hardie

James Hardie and Alice May Shepard were married on April 25, 1909, at Deer Isle, Maine, "in the presence of Mr. Lewis Shepard and Mrs. Lewis," according to the marriage certificate. Alice, born in 1892, was seventeen years old at the time, and Jim was twenty-five. When Jim took up residence as the captain and caretaker of Bear Island in 1910, Alice and their three-month-old daughter, Lillian, born on May 15, 1910, joined him.

Jim had worked for Lewis Shepard before his marriage to Alice. Lewis, now his father-in-law, was working at neighboring islands as a caretaker and would have known that new owners of Bear were looking for a caretaker about the time that Jim and Alice married.

Alice would spend the rest of Jim's life by his side and give birth to six more children, all boys: James Jr., in 1912; Wolcott, 1913; Winslow, 1920; Martin, 1922; Carl, 1925; and Pearl, 1933. According to Jim's immigration and naturalization papers, all the children, with the exception of Lillian, were born on Deer Isle. Lillian was born in Southwest Harbor. Before it was time to give birth, Alice would leave Bear to stay with her relatives on Little Deer Isle.

Little Deer Isle is connected to Deer Isle by a causeway that goes over the clam flats. In 1939, the Deer Isle–Sedgewick Bridge was built over the Eggemoggin Reach, connecting the mainland to Little Deer Isle and Deer Isle. It stands today as evidence of an engineering feat, only one of four built in that design.

Alice would then return as soon as she could with the newborn. She readily adapted to island life on Bear with zest. The family related that Alice said that for one three-year period, she didn't leave the island except for one day.

For all their years on Bear Island, the Harbor House was the Hardies' residence. Located on a peninsula on the northwest point, a small dwelling existed on that site when Caroline Andrews bought Bear Island. With permission from the owners, Jim expanded the small structure there as his family grew, adding bedrooms on the ground floor and a gabled attic on the upper floor. This main house was surrounded by a series of smaller structures, including a workhouse, a hen house, and a small house for smoking meat. The main house had no indoor plumbing, and a coal-burning stove and wood- and driftwood-burning stoves provided heat.

The area of the peninsula with the house and surrounding buildings formed one side of a deep-water harbor, and the point is still known today as Hardie Head. The other side of the harbor was formed by a string of small islets tapering out to what the Hardies called Camp Point. There was a small house at the end of the point where the weir tender would stay. This came to be called Piggie's Point by the summer family. Rosy Fuller Kenison wrote that she named it that way as she used "to play over there in that salt water pool at low tide and there used to be a 'great big pig sty'" there.[21]

Bear's exceptional harbor was a busy working harbor, with a long fisherman's wharf, an outer wharf off of Hardie Head, and

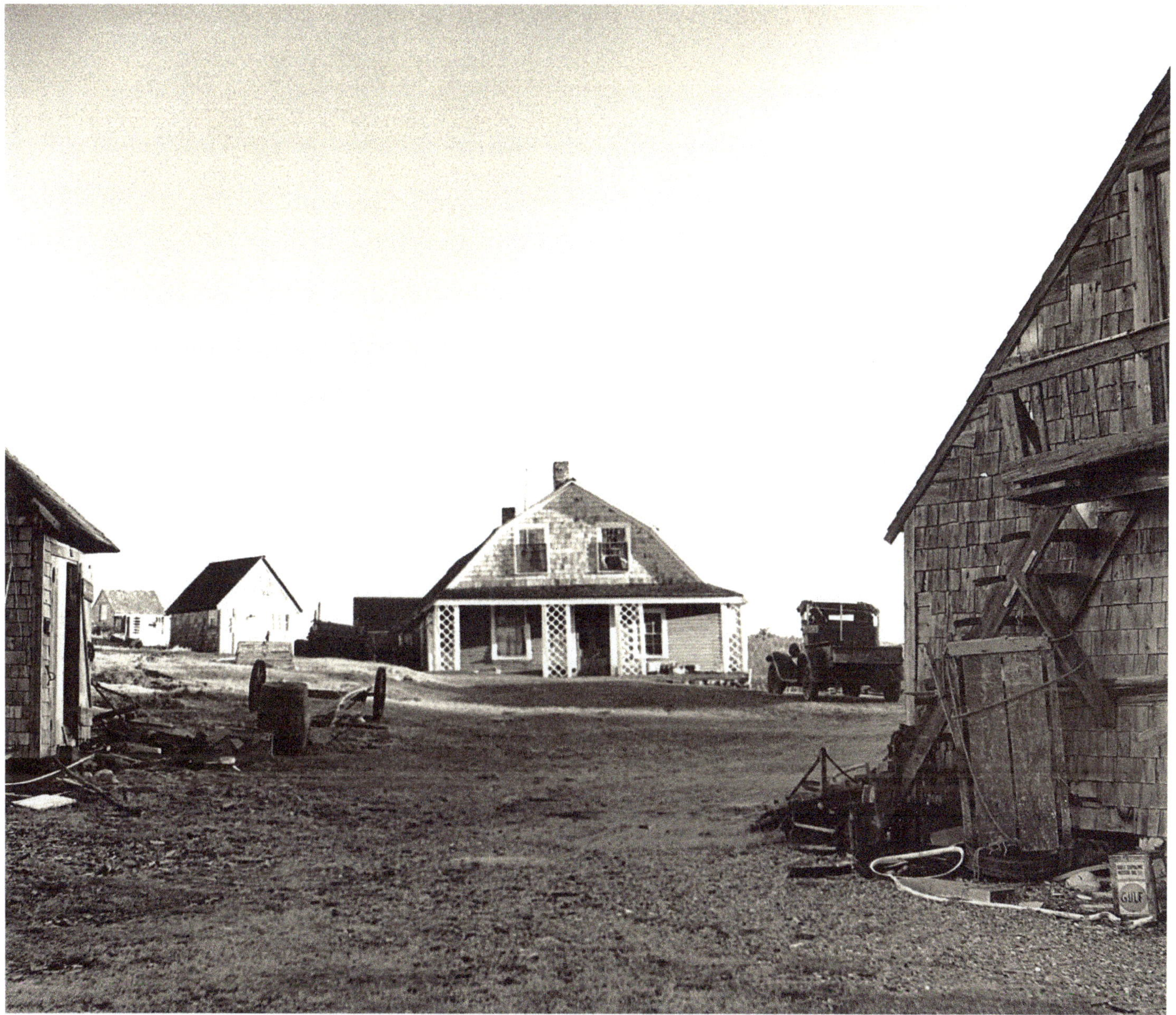

The Harbor House and surroundings; the heart of living and working of the Hardie family on Bear Island, 1940.
GEOFFREY BAKER PHOTO

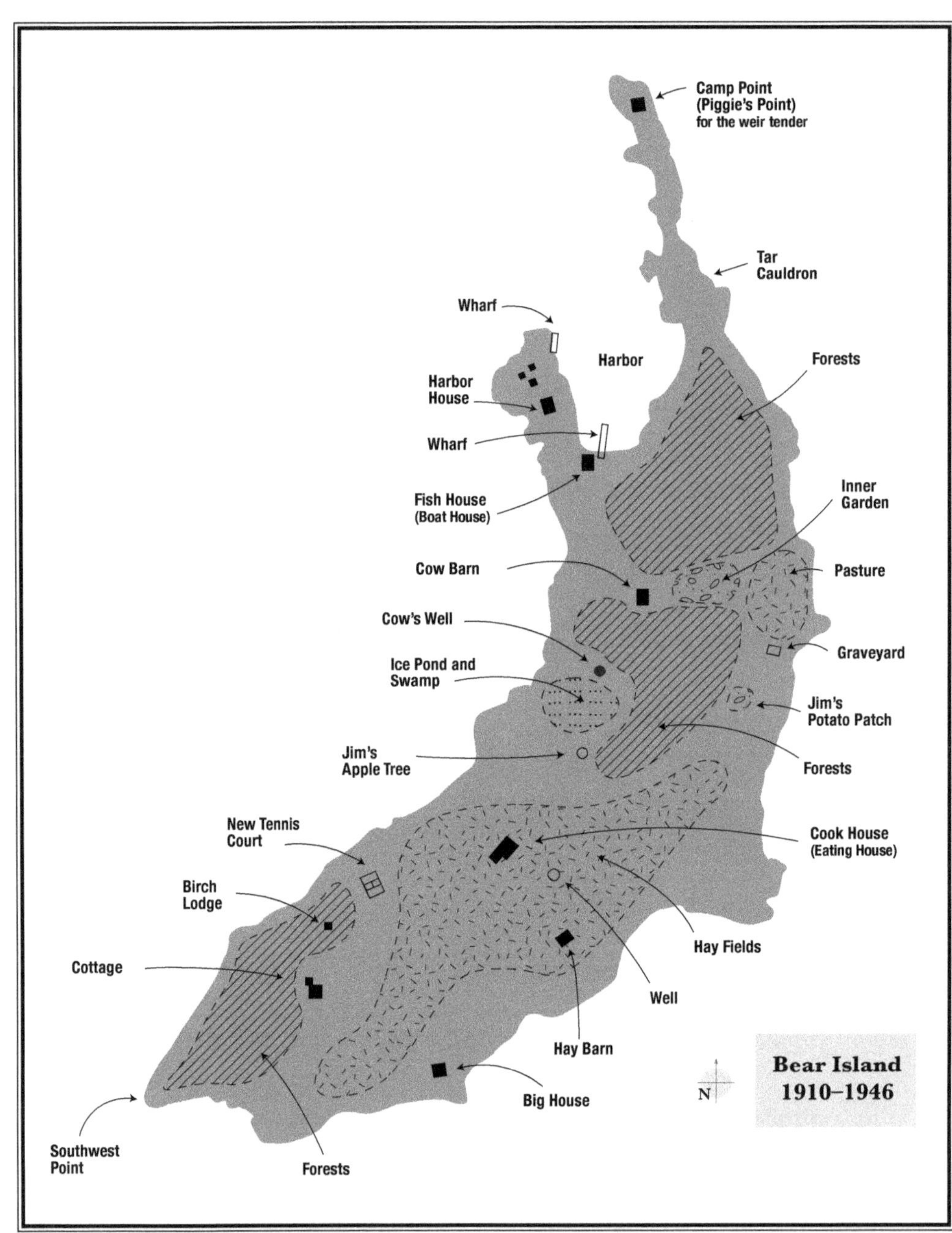

MAP DRAWN BY ISABEL JANE MARVEL

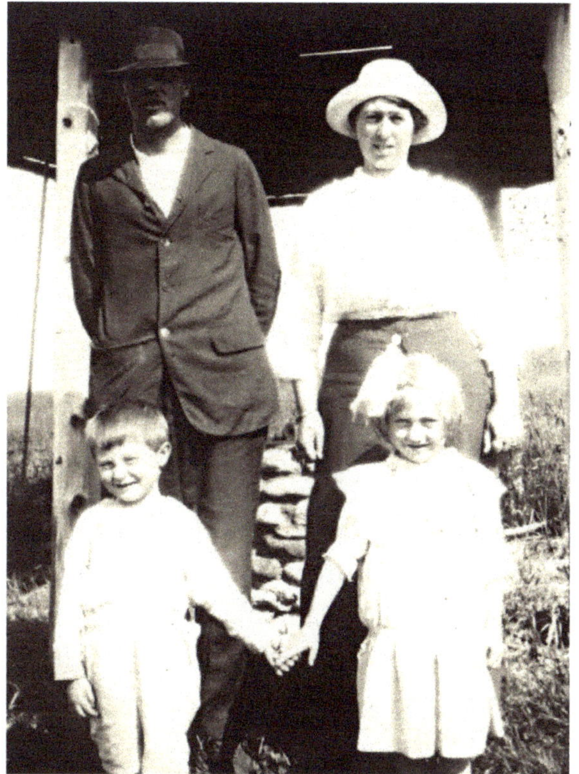

Jim and Alice Hardie and children, James and Lillian, at the well by the Cook House (Eating House), 1915. BEAR ISLAND FAMILY ARCHIVES

Jim's boats and his sons' fishing boats tied up at the wharves or out at moorings. Next to the inner wharf on the shore was what the Hardies called the Fish House, later called the Boat House. The Harbor House, the Fish House (Boat House), and the inner wharf stand today, all vital parts of Bear.

As the Hardie matriarch, Alice was a warm and loving person, and I clearly recall her wonderful, almost boisterous laugh, which would encompass all in the room, as in a large embrace. She must have had prodigious strength, as evidenced by pictures of her cutting ice. That was a job that Jim disliked, as he declared in a February 4, 1916, letter: *"so if it ceaps cold like it is now for a few days i will start to cut the ice, that is the only joB i dread."* Alice was supportive and strong enough to help him out! She also milked the cows, and her three-legged milking stool remains on Bear Island.

Raising and caring for the children took up much of Alice's time, especially when Jim would be fishing off-island, depending on the season. In a June 11, 1917, letter to Wolcott Fuller, he mentioned, *"i have Been verry Bizzy this spring where the times is so hard i have Bin away claming in my Boat i youst to go away monday and stay until satday but now the claming is all over and i am to work farmng."*

Cooking and feeding the family took up much of Alice's time as well. Bread baking was a specialty as well as a necessity. She canned the vegetables grown on the island. She loved to knit, and a Geoffrey Baker picture of 1940 captures her doing just that. Jim kept sheep on Bear Island. Jim and the family, including Alice, rounded up the sheep once a year for shearing. Alice made sweaters and gloves out of the natural, lanolin-infused, thick gray wool. She also "knit" the small netted bait bags for the lobster traps for her family's use. In later years she would sell them as well.

By 1930, Jim also had his own island when he purchased Scrag Island from the Eaton family. Scrag is a five-acre island close by Bear. Jim built a small camp on it for tending his weirs and kept sheep on the island too. After 1946, it would become his and Alice's last home.

Alice had family close by in the Bay. The cluster of neighboring islands provided jobs for the Shepards and the Hardies. The men, like her father, Lewis, worked as caretakers and on small jobs. The women worked as maids or in the kitchens. In addition, Alice's father, Lewis Shepard, served as a caretaker of Great Spruce Head

Island, working for Capt. Monte Green from 1913 to 1917, and then as head caretaker from 1917 until 1925.[22] Prior to that he had lived and worked on Butter Island, serving as a caretaker at the resort called Dirigo Colony. "Lewis Shepard . . . was also a caretaker on Butter Island and lived there with his family from 1908 until 1912."[23] The resort, started at the turn of the twentieth century, housed a casino and hotel accommodating up to one hundred and fifty guests at its peak time, from 1910 to 1915. Abby Shepard Weed, a younger sister of Alice, recalled that she and Alice and the youngest sister, Josie, all worked there in the kitchen.[24] The Hardies and Shepards had a long-standing working relationship with Great Spruce Head, as well.

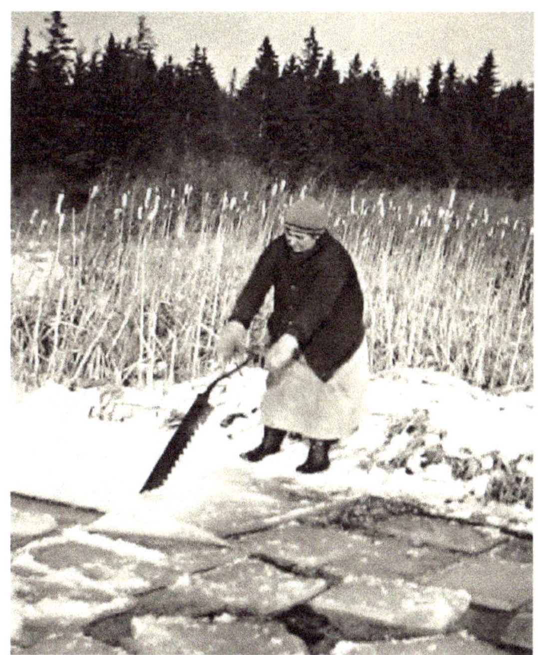

Alice cutting ice in the pond at the swamp, 1939. BEAR ISLAND FAMILY ARCHIVES

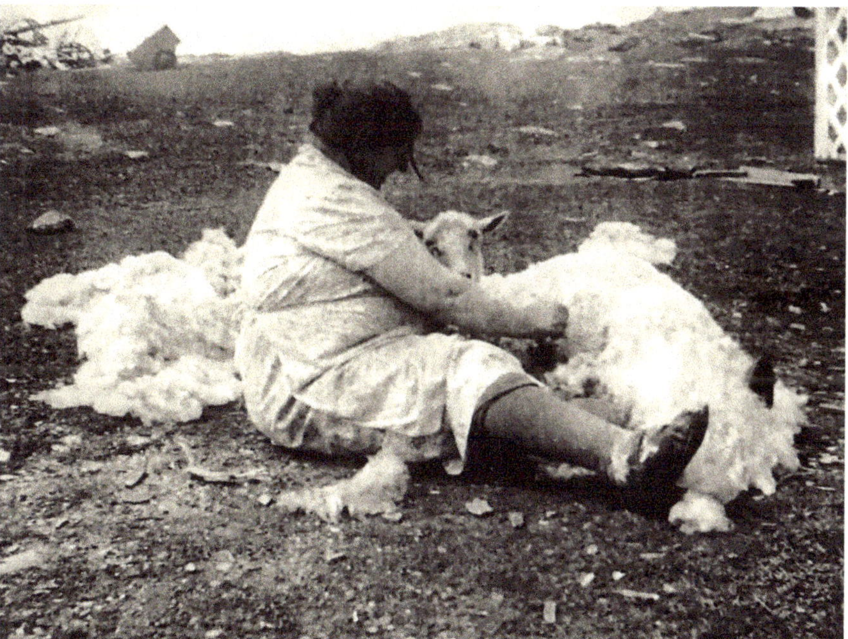

Alice shearing sheep on the lawn at the Harbor House, 1943. BEAR ISLAND FAMILY ARCHIVES

Caretaking became a family tradition for the Hardie family, as it was in the Shepard family. Jim and Alice and their family combined fishing, farming, and caretaking on a year-round basis, a way of life that began to change in the second half of the twentieth century.

Wolcott Hardie, Jim's second-born son, was caretaker of Great Spruce Head from October 1951 until October 1955. After Jim had left Bear Island, Walter Shepard, Josie Shepard's son and Lewis Shepard's grandson, was caretaker of Bear Island from 1948 until 1955. He was then caretaker at Great Spruce Head, like his cousin Wolcott Hardie, from 1955 until 1965. These capable fishermen and caretakers, and their families, helped one another out as well, forming a community of island neighbors.

Jim's letters to the Fuller and King families mention Alice frequently, and he almost always refers to her as "Mrs. Hardie." Today, would she be called co-captain?

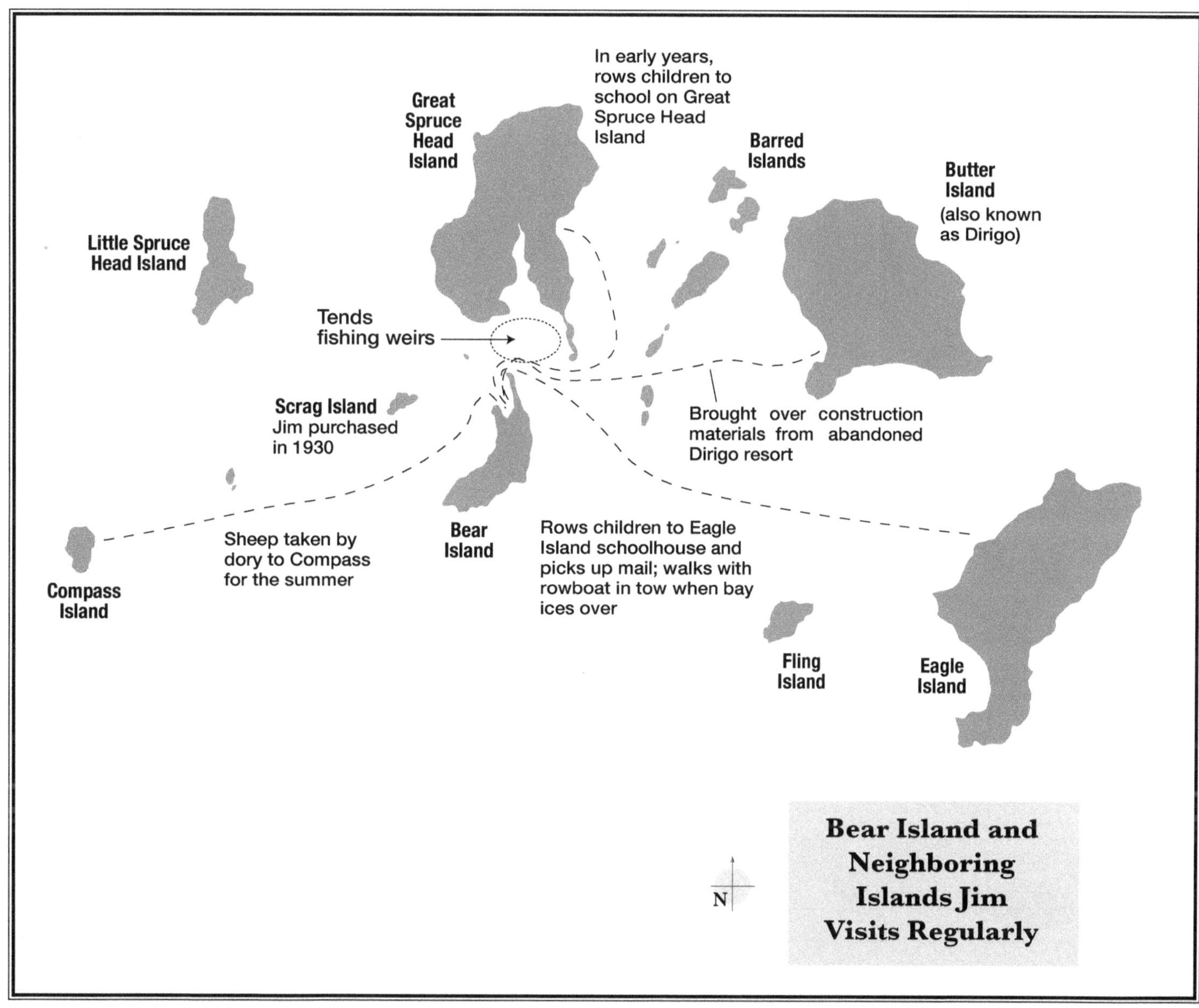

MAP DRAWN BY ISABEL JANE MARVEL

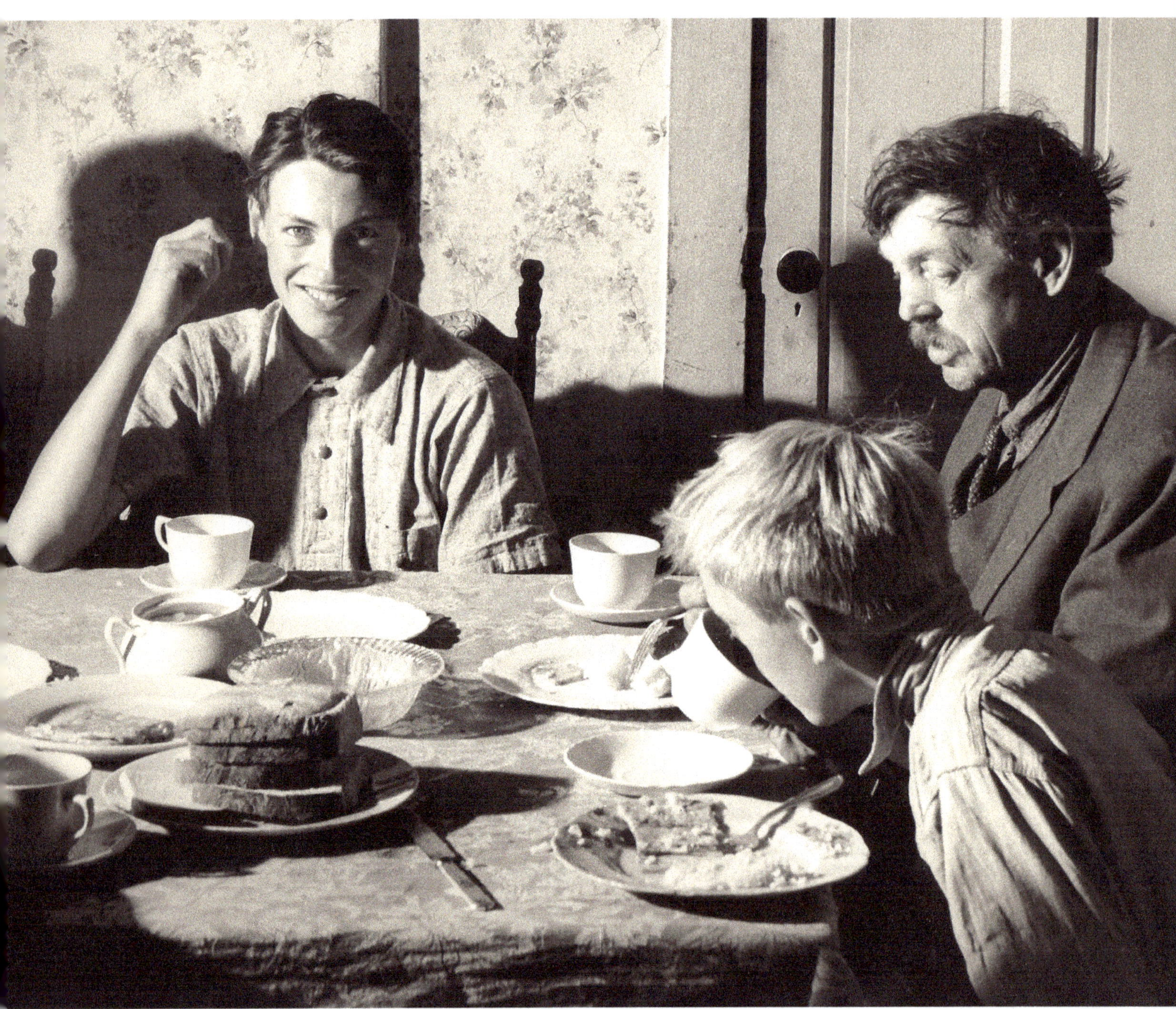

Supper in the Harbor House: Walter Shepard, Jim, and Pearl, 1940. GEOFFREY BAKER PHOTO

Jim and His Children

Jim's children were a major, ever constant presence in his life, and he in theirs. As his family expanded, so did the size of the Harbor House where they lived throughout the year. This close-knit family scenario was a contrast to Jim's early upbringing, that of an orphan sent across the Atlantic to a foster home from which he ran away when he was old enough to go to sea.

As a full-time father, Jim passed on his knowledge and skills to his children, especially his sons. Wolcott Hardie, his second son, recalled that "we were not restricted at any age. If we were able to do it, we did it."[25] Jim considered his main occupation to be that of a fisherman, as he declared on his immigration papers.

Fishing enabled Jim to earn a meager living and feed his family at the same time. He taught his sons to be fishermen as well. They learned how to use fishing lines or nets to catch cod, hake, haddock, mackerel, and sardines. Fishing was seasonal, and depending on the season, the boys learned to set traps and haul for lobsters, drag for scallops, dig and rake for clams at low tide, and harvest mussels. They learned how to set up and care for the weirs, which functioned as large, enclosed nets to catch the smaller sardines and the larger herring.

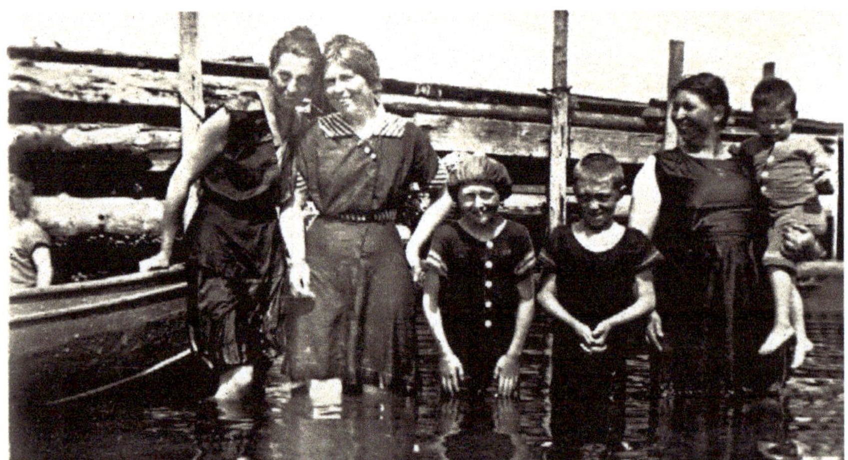

Hardie family and friends swimming in the Harbor, 1918.
BEAR ISLAND FAMILY ARCHIVES

Jim taught his children how to farm and live off the land. The children helped Jim with the tasks on the island, such as working in the gardens, mowing and raking hay in the fields, and collecting firewood. According to a recollection by Wolcott Hardie, there weren't enough trees on the island to provide all their need for firewood, so the family scoured beaches for driftwood, stacking it up in big piles to dry for use as firewood.[26] The sons also recall that they bought a new stove every year because the salt in the driftwood would burn out the stoves. The boys learned to hunt for mink on the land, and large sea birds on the shores, all of which were a source of food.

Schooling was a major activity for the children. This required a commute to neighboring islands, with Jim rowing them back and forth. They started off their schooling at Great Spruce Head for two years while there was a sufficient number of children to warrant a schoolteacher. "Capt. Lamont 'Monty' Green, caretaker of Great Spruce Head Island, had three children, and there were two or three children on Bear Island."[27] After Great Spruce Head, the children attended school at neighboring Eagle Island, where the schoolhouse still stands.

Starting in 1910, the State of Maine regulated the education system for land in unorganized territories like those in Hancock County, including the "five-pupil minimum" requirement for a teacher to be appointed by the state. On Eagle Island, school enrollment ranged from five to thirteen students, as there were a number of full-time residents on Eagle, including the lighthouse keeper and his family. The teacher lived on Eagle Island, and the Hardie children boarded on that island during the week. The State of Maine made a small contribution to children who had to board away from their homes in order to go to school.[28]

Weather was a big determinant in school attendance. In an early letter of January 20, 1918, addressed to Caroline Fuller, Jim wrote, *"in regards to scool wich you spoke about some time ago   we are haven no scool this winter and i am in one way verry glad of it   But i am agoin to see what i can do in regards to it next summer."*

In an April 13, 1919, letter, he reported, *"lillian and James is at school at eagel island."* On February 7, 1926, Jim writes, *"the children is at scool oll winter this winter But they are home today and i am agoing to take theme Bake to eagel tonight   the children is very bissy eating ice cream wich we have Just frose a freaser full and they are enJoying themselves very much at it."*

By the fall of 1926, Lillian, the oldest child, had left home. Jim reported in a January 9, 1927, letter that *"lillian got thrue the eagel island school and now she is gon out to work she is clurk in a store at south Blue hill and i had her home for a weak and a half for crmx and we oll enJoyed our self very much lillian has Bin working since octoBer the first and she likes it very much."*

In the same letter Jim wrote that *"i had oll my children home for crmx hollowdays you no that the 3 Boys gos to school at eagel now James and wolcott and winslow."*

At some point the children started going to school on Deer Isle, boarding with Alice's family in Mountainville, in the town of Deer

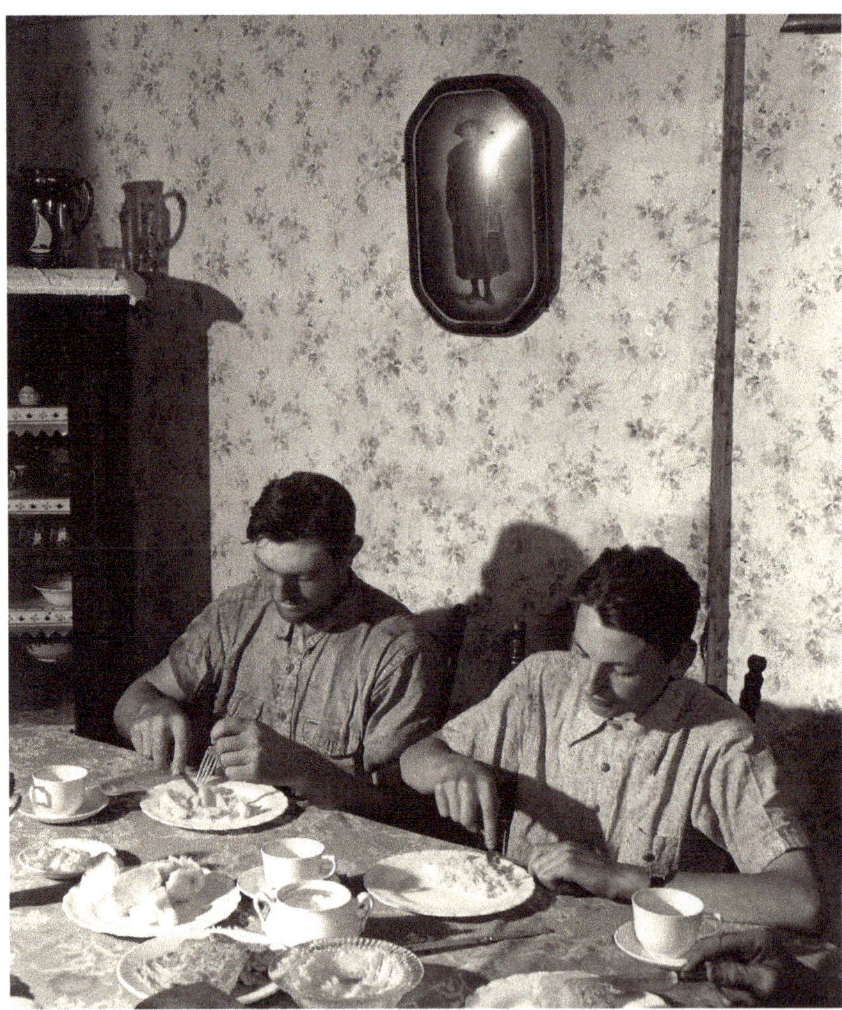

Supper in the Harbor House, 1940. GEOFFREY BAKER PHOTO

Isle on Deer Isle.[29] Depending on the weather, Jim would bring them home for the weekend. With the children all away at school, Jim wrote on December 10, 1928, that he and Alice would also live in Sunset on Deer Island for a few winter months. *"mrs Hardie and i stayed until christmas last year and then we move to sunset for the winter."*

In a January 14, 1934, letter Jim reported: *"James lives over to sunset Deer island he had a Boy Baby Born this fall and he feals verry*

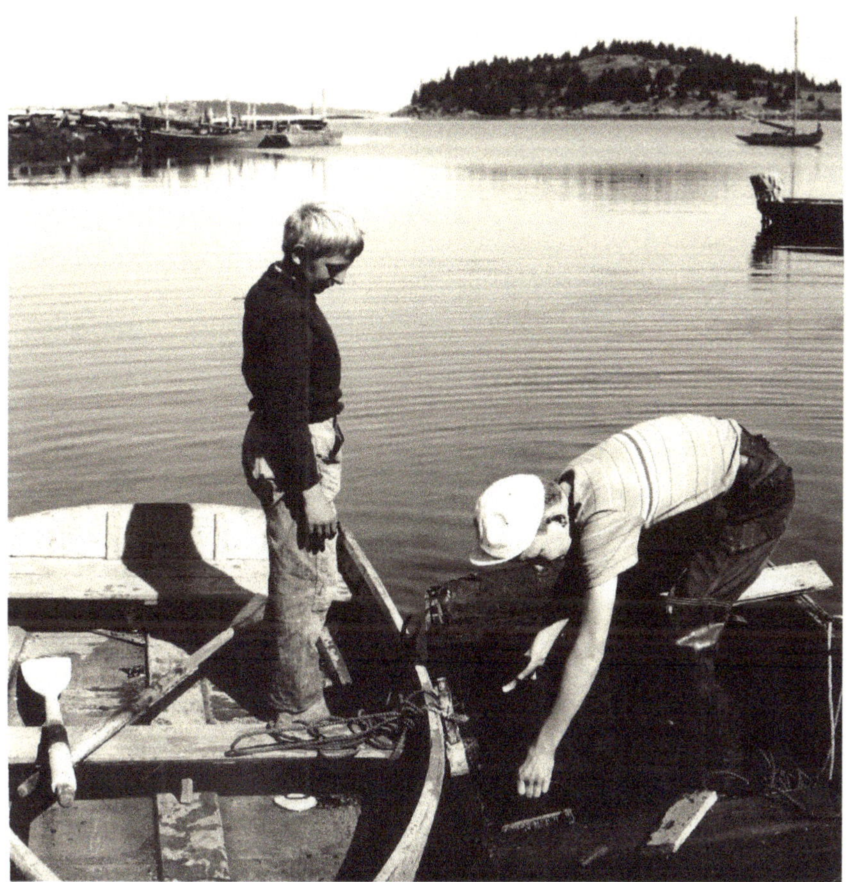

Pearl and older relative on skiffs at the dock in the Harbor, 1940.
GEOFFREY BAKER PHOTO

proud of it." In a December 29, 1934, letter to Wolcott Fuller, Jim wrote about difficult winter weather, saying, *"well i will be taking the children Back to Deer island to school the first chance."*

Living on an island and making a living from the sea dictated travel by sea. The children grew up on the water. Often the weather would change from the time Jim would leave for the mainland to the time he returned. His letter of January 28, 1924, to Wolcott describes such a trip. He wrote:

> *i was over to camden last monday i left home i had farly good weather there was a little west wind when i got over to Job island Bar the western bay was feather wite and it was Just zero then and when i got into camden the general knox was all sheaded over with ice   the spray wood fly over her and freas as fast as it came over her Belive me wolcott the old general knox will go to windred as long as we can look to windred By the time i was redy for home again it came snow squales from the west and Blowed a liven gal   well i started for home and Beleve me there was some sea aBout   that time i csme from camden warfs to Bear island warf in 74 minutes Josie and Jamsey and Kimbel and lewie was with me and the Bravest man i had was Jamsey But i tel you Josie was very scared But the general knox run like a bird on a wing*

Jim described a trip home from Belfast in a February 7, 1926, letter to Wolcott:

> *it Bloed offel hard from the north west and made a sweft run home for my crue   i had Jamesey and wolcott and wolcott sed when we comed out of Belfasr that it was the hardes wind he was ever out in and i asked them if they felt scared and they sead no so i let come for home so we made the trip oll ok*

As the children grew older and left home to lead their own lives, go to school, work, and raise their families, Jim and Alice would correspondingly spend more time in the winters on Deer Isle. Without his sons around to help as Jim grew older too, the caretaking work became more of a challenge, as letters quoted in later chapters illustrate.

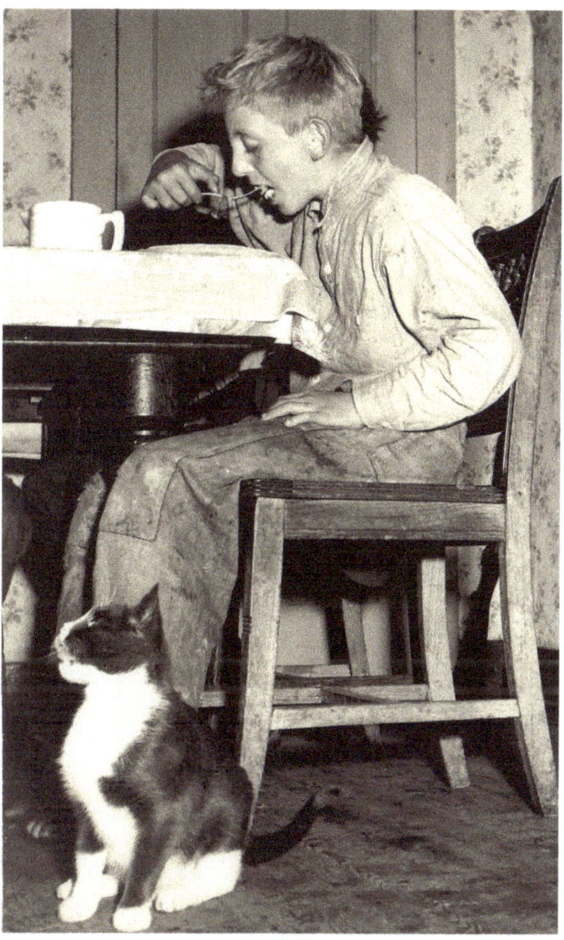

Pearl and cat at supper in the Harbor House, 1940. GEOFFREY BAKER PHOTO

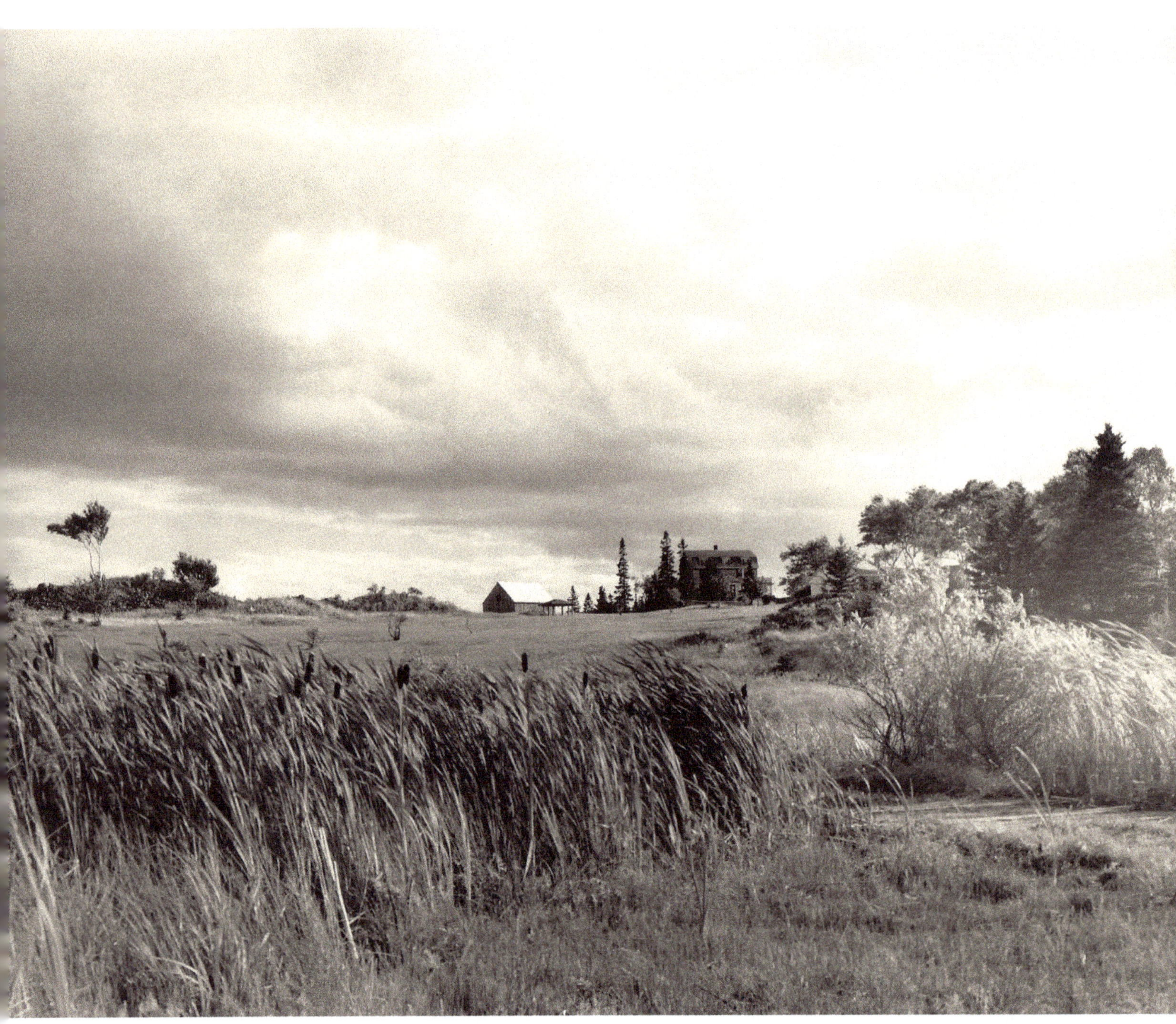

View of the road through the swamp, heading toward the well, the Hay Barn, and the Big House, 1940.
GEOFFREY BAKER PHOTO

Jim's Role in the Lives of the Fuller Children

In 1910, shortly after Mrs. Andrews and her family started to summer on Bear, Richard B. Fuller, the husband of Caroline Andrews Fuller, died. From that time on, Jim took on a major role, that of a father figure and a mentor, in the lives of three of the four young Fuller children: Bucky (Buckminster), Wolcott, and Rosy (Rosamond). Leslie, the oldest sister and a young adult of eighteen years, did not spend as much time on the island as they did. A special bond developed between Jim and the three younger ones. At that time they were fifteen, twelve, and five years of age. Jim often writes in his letters of his affection for the children and would mention how much he was looking forward to the summer, when the family would be there. Jim wrote on February 4, 1916:

> *well wilcott i will Bring this to a close for thise time and hopen to here from you soon again i love to here from you it makes me think of summer when i here from you i will Be glad when summer comes again so we can get together again*

Jim's duties as year-round caretaker expanded in the summertime, to spend time with the summer children. Jim taught the young Fuller offspring and their cousins all about the sea, the tides, the wind, boats, and sailing. Jim's only instruments were his eyes, his wristwatch, his compass, and his formidably retained marine and climate information and knowledge. With little schooling himself, he taught the children from his personal experience.

Wolcott Fuller said that he received all his learning and love of the sea from Jim. He became a great seaman, sailor, and navigator himself. At the age of twenty, Wolcott was the quartermaster on troop ships sailing from the United States to North Africa during World War I. Wolcott was the navigator on the winning boat of two Newport-to-Bermuda races in the 1930s, including the overall winner of 1932, John G. Alden's *Malabar X*. He remained in the US Navy Reserve after World War I and headed to Boston when World War II broke out, to be in charge of the Navigation School at the Boston Navy Yard. He was later transferred to the Bar Harbor Naval Base in 1943 as adjunct commander.

Jim and Wolcott had a special affection for one another, a friendship that lasted till Jim's death. Jim named his second son after my father. Alice Hardie wrote to Caroline Fuller on January 2, 1916: *"i hav Just arrived from my mothers and brat with me a young sun that was Borned December 13, and he waid 12½ when he was washed a breast and my huben named him Welcott Edward."*

Wolcott's elder brother, Buckminster, acknowledged the lasting influence and mentorship role of Jim Hardie in his own life's work. He wrote in 1967:

> Few men affected Bucky Fuller's early life to greater extent than did Jim Hardie, because of Jim's sailorman's skill with boats and his vast physical drive to build and his innate urge for self-teaching. Having no known mother of his own Jim competed with Bucky for favor in Mrs. Fuller's (Bucky's mother) [*sic*] eyes,

for as mistress of the Island she was also the Island family's mother. Jim also competed with Bucky because Bucky had "schooling." Bucky competed with Jim because he was so physically strong and was so rich in sea lore and fundamental skills.[30]

Rosy Fuller Kenison, who grew up to be a fine sailor also, wrote in 1971 to one of Wolcott Fuller's granddaughters:

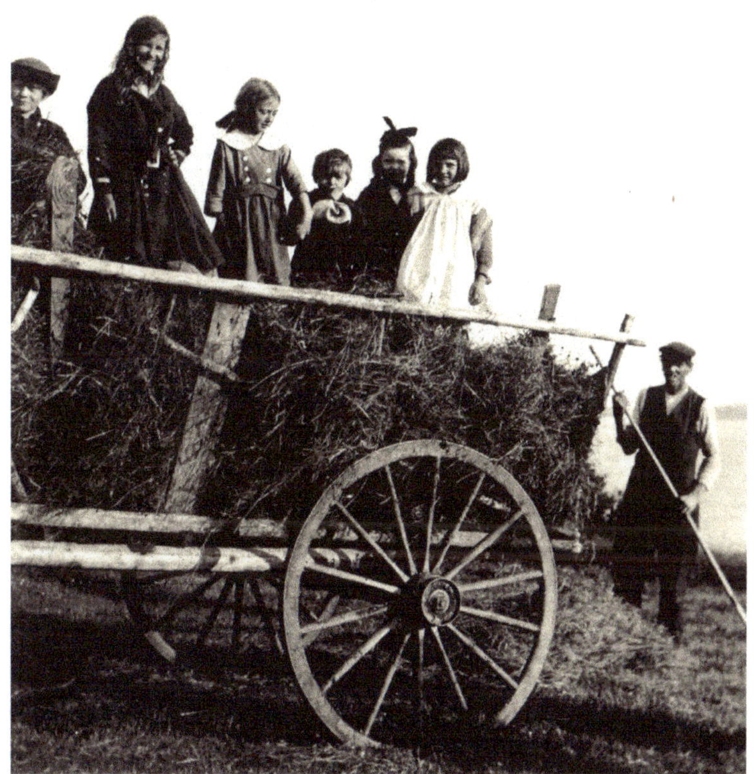

Jim raking hay by the Big House, with Hardie, Fuller, and King children playing in the hay wagon, 1916.
BEAR ISLAND FAMILY ARCHIVES

No telling of the Island would be complete without telling about Jim Hardie. . . . Mother took him on. . . . He was a great man and brought me up and if it weren't for him, none of us would be going to the island now. He was a great sailor, amazing in the fog, knew the bottom of the Bay like a book from scalloping to lobstering, was a carpenter, a farmer, a philosopher, engines were the only thing that frustrated him. He loved your grandfather and that is why he named his second son after him.[31]

Jim appreciated any communication and gesture from the family. My father regularly sent Jim a subscription to a Boston newspaper.[32] In a letter to Wolcott on January 3, 1917, he wrote:

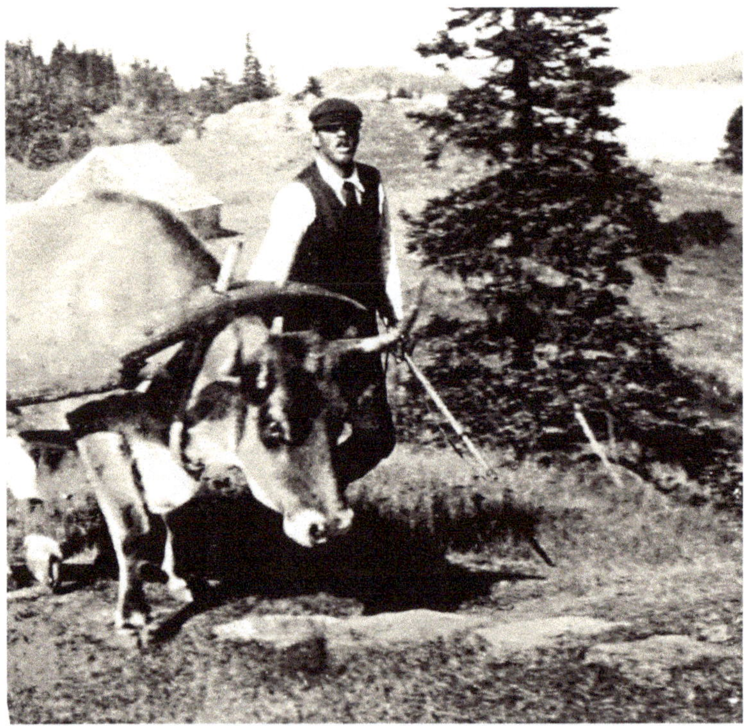

Billy, the ox, and Jim at the Big House, 1921.
BEAR ISLAND FAMILY ARCHIVES

well you say you re sending me the papers and i thank you verry
much i think it is offel good of you i hope i shall be abel to do as
much for you some time. . . . hopes to here from you soon again

As much as Jim expressed his affection for the children, he freely expressed his expectations that Wolcott would keep in touch, even during the time of World War I, when both Bucky and Wolcott joined the war effort. On June 11, 1917, Jim wrote:

well wolcott i here that you have Bin doun to Bar harBor and
found the wego i was verry much soprised when i herd that you
was down there and did not get to see us i hope that you will get
here and see us when you come down again

The *Wego* was the family boat that was commissioned as a patrol boat, the USS *Wego*, at the time of that war. Both Bucky and Wolcott formed part of the crew, Bucky as captain and Wolcott as deck hand.

In a letter to their mother of January 20, 1918, Jim wrote:

i now drop you a few lines in ancer to yours of decemBer 19 and
was glad to hear from you in regards to the Boys i am very glad
that Bucky has a good Boat for the petrol Bisness i got a letter
from him a few days ago and i was glad to here from him but i
have not herd from wolcot this winter i wood rite him if i no
where to rite

Wolcott did write, and Jim replied on March 24, 1918:

in ancer to yours of February 17 wich i just receved last week and
was very glad to here form you there has in a month that i cood
not get to eagel for my mail that is the rason that i did not get
your letter Before But the ice is oll out from around the island

and i tell you i am offel glad ot it for i have not bin eany father
than eagel island for 2 months and a half

That letter Jim finished with a little scolding: *"hopes to hear from*
you soon again i didnt no why you did not rite to me Before hopen that
you will do beter this time."

This was during the period that Wolcott was serving as a quartermaster on troop ships going across the Atlantic Ocean to North
African ports. On January 12, 1919, Jim wrote:

in ancer to yours of novemBer 30, 1918 in wich i was verry glad
to here from you wich i see that you are a long ways from home
well wolcot glad to here you say that you will Be on the island
next summer for you seam to Be the maine stay here at the island
in the summer

As the boys grew older, their time spent on the island was lim-
ited. Jim wrote to Wolcott on December 12, 1923:

well wolcot i am offel glad for you that you have a good JoB and
like it i think it is Better to have a JoB and Be working hard
then to Be worren where he is going to get a JoB you shourly must
of struck a streak of luck well wolcot i mist you verry much of not
Being hear to the island this sumer But i no Just how it was with
you you wanted work and if you had com you wood of had that
worren on your mind But wolcot i sopose you will get a little
vackshen next sumer

In a May 23, 1927, letter, Jim wrote:

well wolcot things is fine at the island and i hopes you will try
and get to the island this summer for the little wile i wood like to
see you get here well wolcot how re you getting along with your

Bissness i hope you are getting along all right   i here you are in chacago now

Clearly the mutual feelings of respect and affection established during the early years between Jim and the Fuller children would serve to buttress the difficult times that ensued during the late thirties between Jim and other owners.

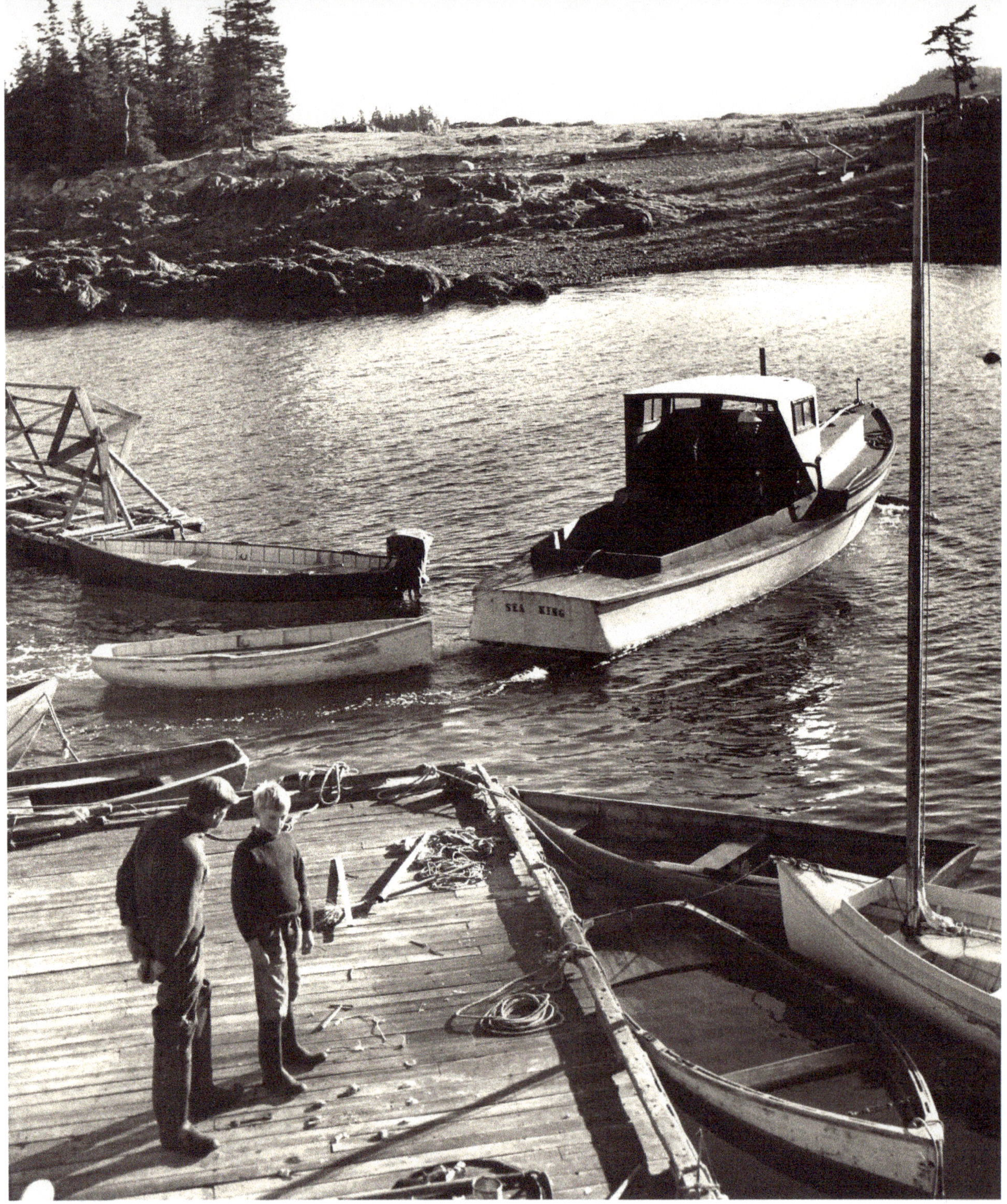

Jim and Pearl on the dock at the Harbor at low tide, 1940.   GEOFFREY BAKER PHOTO

Jim's Presence

Jim was by all accounts an impressive figure. Bucky remembered him as "a six foot one inch lean Scot . . . eyes permanently blood-shot by exposure to the Antarctic Sun." He continued:

> [Jim] had a most extraordinary and uncanny intuition and logic as well as a gargantuan will and muscular strength to accomplish. He felt competitive with the rest of the Penobscot Bay people, to whom he was an outsider. He out-clammed, out-scalloped, and out-fished them all. In one winter he dug and shelled out 80 barrels of clams with his own hands.[33]

Rosy, in a letter about the history of the island, quoted her mother, Mrs. Fuller, as saying, "He was very scary looking, a big brawny man with huge hands and bloodshot eyes from being many years at sea on sealing vessels."[34]

Although I was young and did not spend extended stays at the island until after World War II, I remember Jim clearly and dearly. He was by then living on Scrag Island and no longer employed at Bear. However, he continued to do special jobs upon request and would come by the harbor frequently. My sense of him then was of a person of superior, trustworthy capability around the water. I was impressed by this large man, dressed up for work, who spoke with a Scottish accent and seemed to know so much, and of whom my father and mother seemed so fond. There was a personal magnetism about him and handsomeness.

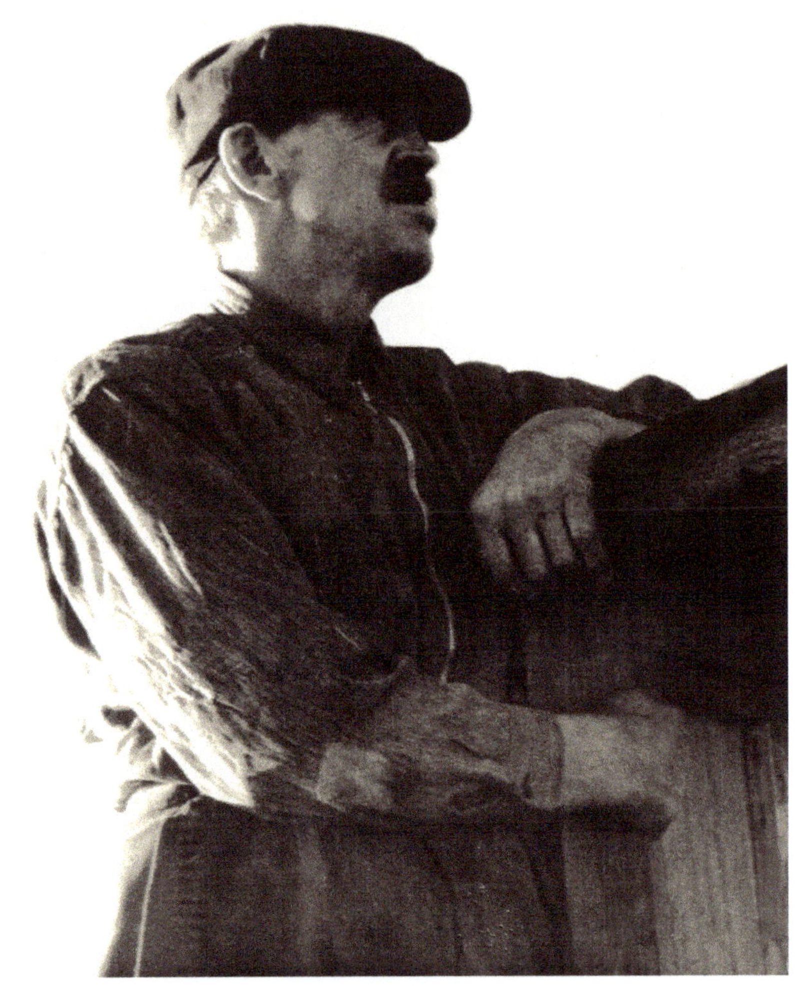

Jim on his boat, 1940. GEOFFREY BAKER PHOTO

Jim paid attention to his attire, reflecting a sense of pride in his job as caretaker and captain of the *Wego*. Pictures show Jim often wearing a necktie and a vest while at work on the island, and always a hat. In a February 25, 1917, letter, Jim thanks Wolcott for sending him a hat *"and it is a dandie on me and just what i nead for this cind of a winter."* In another letter of April 13, 1919, he thanks Wolcott for a suit. *"olso i receved the sut of close wich you sent me and was verry pleased of them . . . they are just my fit and i thank you very much for them . . . eanny thing like that you no is very exceptel to me."*

Jim radiated strength even when he was older and stooped by work. Sporting a mustache, he usually wore boots in addition to the ubiquitous hat. The last picture I have of Jim was taken the summer before he died, in 1953, aboard his boat, tied up at the wharf at the harbor on Bear. He is slightly stooped, wearing a hat and suspenders.

Alice described him as good-looking even in death. She wrote to Wolcott Fuller on November 24, 1954, shortly after Jim died: *"well wolcott, Jim look nice of when he was lay out   if you see him you word say he was about 30 years old."*

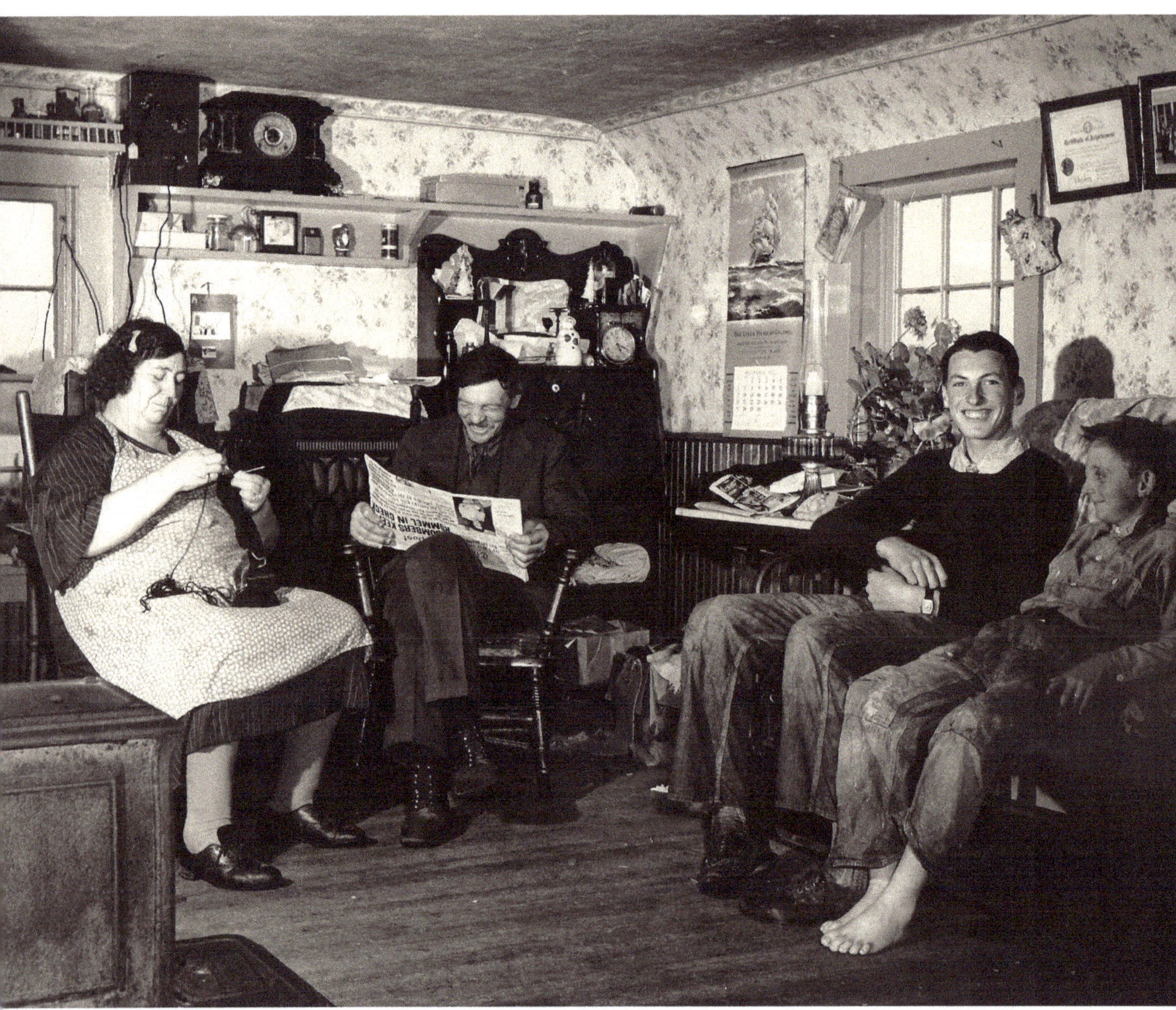

Alice, Jim, Walter Shepard, and Pearl, gathering before supper at the Harbor House, 1940. GEOFFREY BAKER PHOTO

Jim's Wit

Jim's letters reveal his dry sense of humor. The few instances of purposeful wittiness often serve as a poignant contrast to the "hard times" narrative of the letters. With his humor, he allowed himself to participate in a little gossip as well. Jim wrote on February 4, 1916, about the caretaker on Great Spruce Head Island, who was going through marital problems. *"simpney boy is on great sproos head yet . . . he has got his bil from his wife now and he is honting for a nother wife now he is just a silly as ever."*

After naming his second son after Wolcott Fuller, who was eighteen at the time, Jim wrote on March 6, 1916, *"well wilcot you are quite a lot older then when you left here for you are unkil wilcot now."* About another family member, Jim wrote in the same letter that *"my father in law dond stay with me winters you cood not give him money enofe to stay on here in the winter."*

Jim enlarged the Harbor House several times to accommodate the growing family, adding bedrooms and a second floor. In a letter of March 4, 1923, to Mrs. King and Mrs. Fuller, he mentioned his wife, Alice, who was a large woman:

well i am still working at the house and i am very pleased of the
house and also mrs hardie is   of corse you no it takes lots of room
for mrs hardie to get around when she is so little

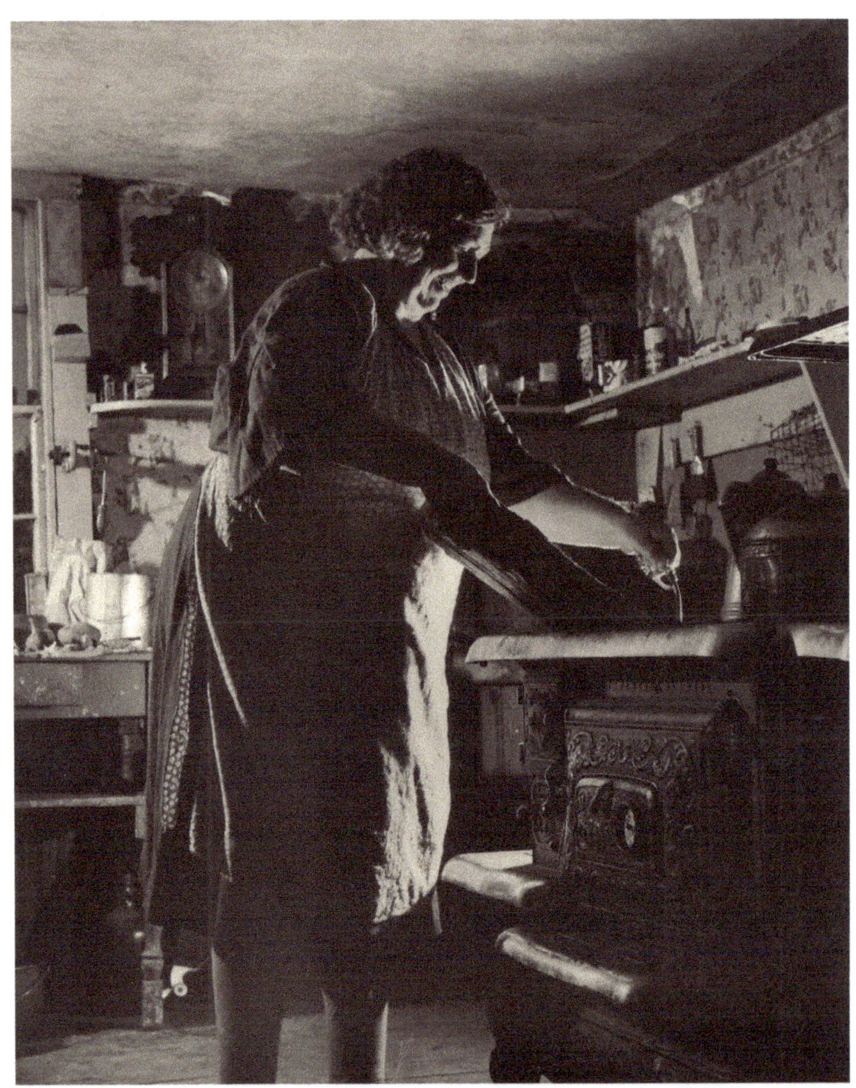

Alice at the stove at the Harbor House, 1940. GEOFFREY BAKER PHOTO

The March 4, 1923, letter also describes a particularly cold winter, with the harbor freezing over and trapping the boats. He wrote about his boat, the *Osprey*, which he had to saw to release from the ice: *"the way it looks and seams to us here that we wood not ger her out to have a sail Before the 4 of July   But i ges it will do a little Better than that."*

Jim wrote to Wolcott on January 28, 1924, about coming plans for the summer involving Wolcott's boat, the *Giddy Gaddy*:

well wolcott i hope to sea you here to the island nex summer and when now you are coming down for your vackshen let me no in time and i will have your Boat oll ready for the water and then you can youse her as soon as you get here and then you may get a chance to sell her   you no it is easer to sell a Boat when she is in the water then when she is on the Bank

In a November 19, 1925, letter he commented: *"well wolcot Josie and mrs Hardie and i inJoying of a good time in Springfeld thrue the radio."* Josie Shepard was Alice Hardie's younger sister; she and her son, Walter Shepard, lived at the Harbor House.

Jim also used his humor to make light of dire fishing conditions, writing on June 6, 1933, *"well wolcott this is offel hard times--- there isent a thing around to do cant as much as catch eanny fish guess they have gon out on a strike."*

One wonders if Jim's wittiness, as revealed in his letters, would also have been the case in his spoken conversations.

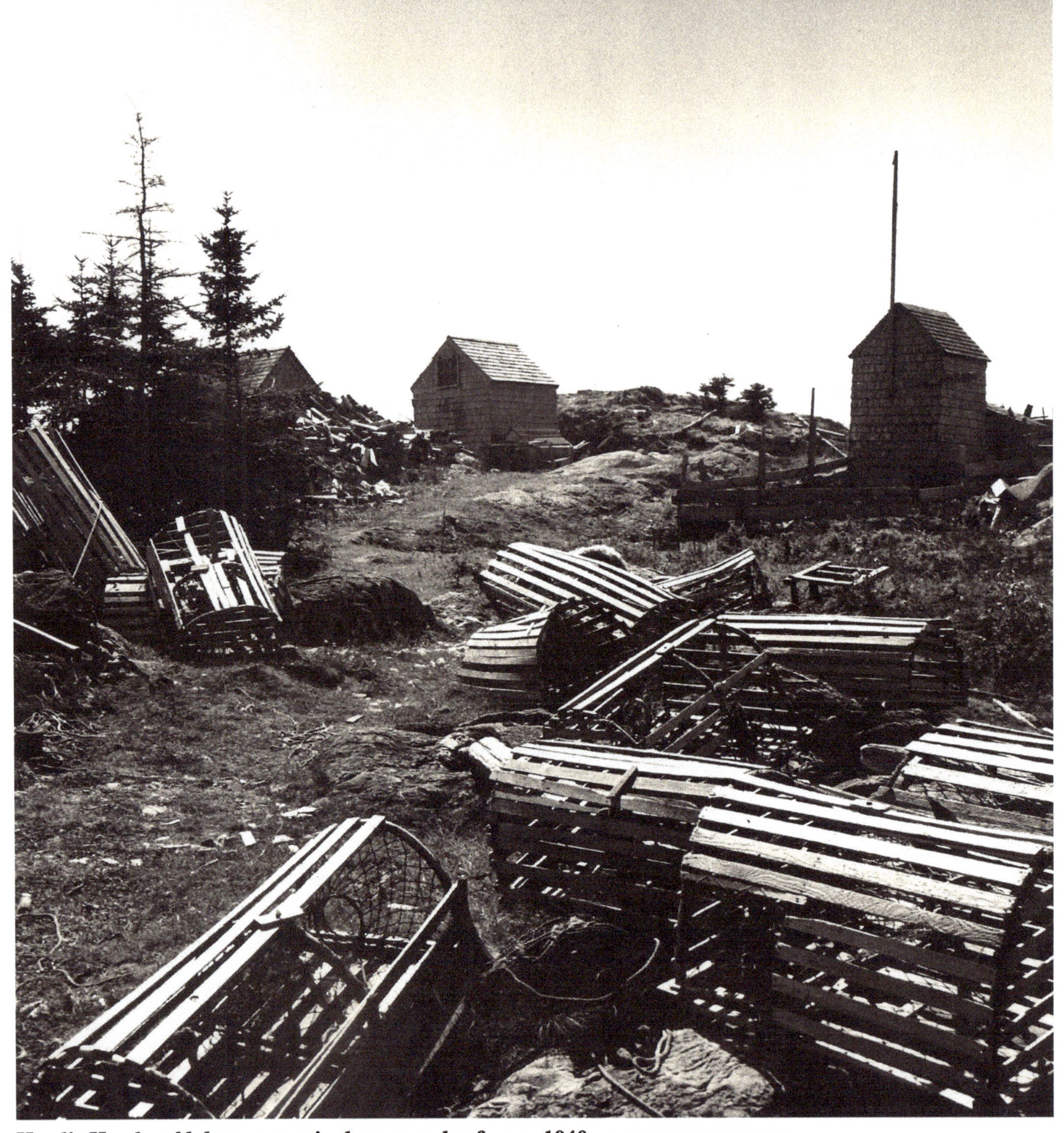

Hardie Head and lobster traps in the outer wharf area, 1940. GEOFFREY BAKER PHOTO

Jim's Management, Work Ethic, and Honesty

Jim took pride in his work and had a strong sense of what was correct, appropriate, and called for in his job as Captain Hardie. Although there are few examples of Jim's commenting critically of others, he did write on March 24, 1918:

> *i had to go to great sproos head eavry day for capten green left*
> *ther and went to Dear isl   he staded over there 2 months   i don't*
> *think that is very good way to take care of a place do you*

There was a lot to plan for, manage, and carry out—and all the while anticipating his employers' wish list for whatever special task he would be asked to do. And Jim would do everything asked. To my knowledge there was no contract with his employers. Instructions and requests arrived by letter from September to June, usually from Caroline Fuller and Lucy King, representing the two branches of the family. It was a relationship of mutual trust.

Jim's son Pearl and daughter-in-law Evelyn related that "when Jim was asked if he knew how to do something, he would say no, but when he started out he knew how to do things." As an example, they mentioned Jim's carpentry skills. One anecdote they liked to tell was that of the Harbor House. Jim had asked Caroline Fuller for permission to add on to the house in order to meet the space needs of his growing family. Mrs. Fuller replied that he could do this as long as he didn't make it too tall to spoil the view of the harbor from the higher parts of the island.

Pearl and Evelyn, as well as Wolcott Hardie, all mention that Jim used wood salvaged from the abandoned buildings of the shuttered Dirigo Resort on Butter Island after World War I in the expansion of the Harbor House. As Wolcott Hardie said, "People helped themselves to what was left, not letting things go to waste." According to *Islands of the Mid-Coast Maine Penobscot Bay:*

> Whole buildings were carried away, some to Deer Isle. . . . The larger buildings such as the Casino were dismantled in orderly fashion . . . parts of the lumber went to build a barn on Eagle and part to construct a house for James Hardie, Lewis Shepard's son-in-law on Bear Island.[35]

Jim must have received a request to provide an estimate for doing renovation work on the Cottage, one of the old nineteenth-century farmhouses standing on the island in 1904, when Mrs. Andrews purchased it. He responded with a well-thought-out economic proposal, based on his assurance that the job would be "done honest" and "what is done will be done right." On October 22, 1934, he wrote:

> *well wolcot in regards to the cotteg i should think it wood tak*
> *Between 2 to 3 hundret dolors But to seperate the estmashen from*
> *inside and out side it is impossoBel   But By doing the work it*
> *can Be ceap seprat when get done   But one thing aBout it*
> *wolcot if i do it it will Be don onest   i wood rather then to take*
> *and i will use everything that is fit to use But have no rotten wood*

that is the reasen i cant tell Just the cost for i dont no aBout the flor Beams until i start and get the flor up and i think in regards to the plaster   i will Be aBel to patch it and mak it look verry good   and in regards to the roof there is some parts of the roof that the shingels has Bin rotted so long that i think some of the Bordes will Be rotted   if so will place in new   But what is don will Be don rite

Managing survival on the island for himself and his family, as well as meeting the caretaker's tasks, required planning out the use of his time as well as that of his children. Hardie's sons Wolcott and Winslow mention helping their father on many a job. In addition to fishing and farming with their father, they helped him carry out the jobs required of caretaking. The island had to be ready to meet the needs of the summer family by the time they arrived. This would

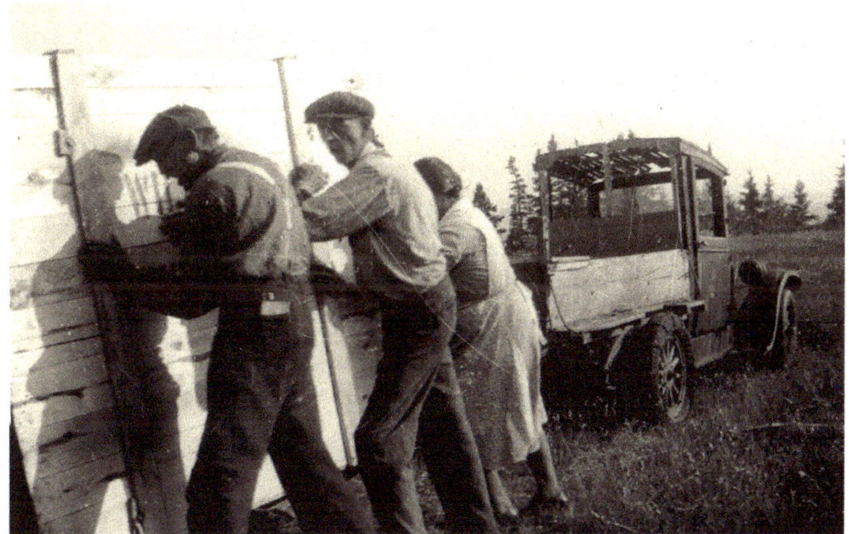

Boarding up: preparing buildings for the winter season; Jim, a son, and Alice, 1943. BEAR ISLAND FAMILY ARCHIVES

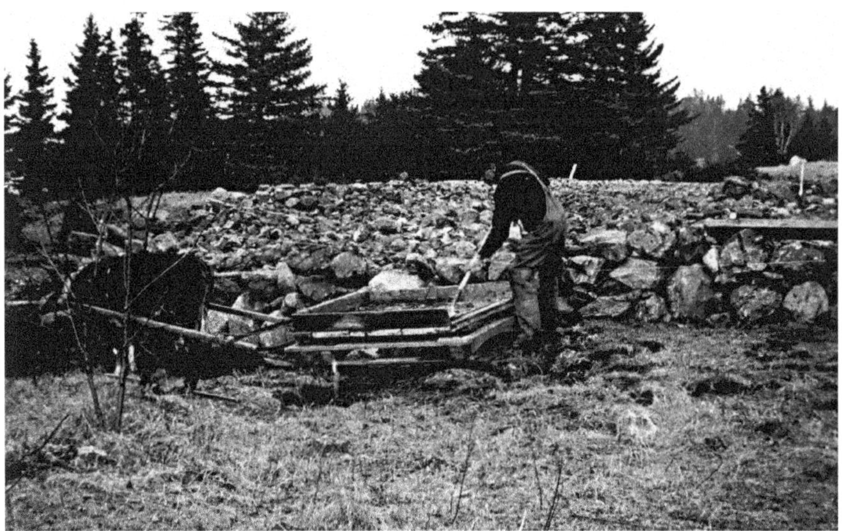

Jim unloading boulders to build up the tennis court foundation, 1942. BEAR ISLAND FAMILY ARCHIVES

include ongoing attention to building and improving the road to get from the harbor to the southern area where the family lived, so that wagons could be pulled with supplies and luggage. Yearly jobs required cutting ice in big chunks from the pond and storing them in sawdust in the Ice House next to the Eating House. Special jobs were asked of Jim and sons, such as building a tennis court, which they started in the 1930s, laying out a stone and boulder foundation. When finished years later as an all-weather clay court, using clay from the island, it was well built and is still in use.

Cisterns, which always seemed to be leaking, were required at the Big House, the Eating House, and the Cottage. Roof gutters, essential to collect run-off rainwater, needed repairs every year. The summer family kept boats, which had to be ready for sailing or motoring by the time the family arrived. Paths required mowing and upkeep. In his springtime letters, Jim also mentioned getting the gardens ready for Lucy King and Caroline Fuller, as he knew they loved the gardens, especially Lucy King. In a letter to her of April 20, 1925, Jim writes that *"in regards to the seads you spoke aBout i have them on hand now all redy to plant as soon as i think they are safe from frost."* The gardens at the Big House, surrounded by stonewalls, are remnants of Jim's work under Aunt Lucy's guidance. The elm trees planted at her request stand majestically tall today and can be seen from a ten-mile radius as one approaches Bear Island by sea.

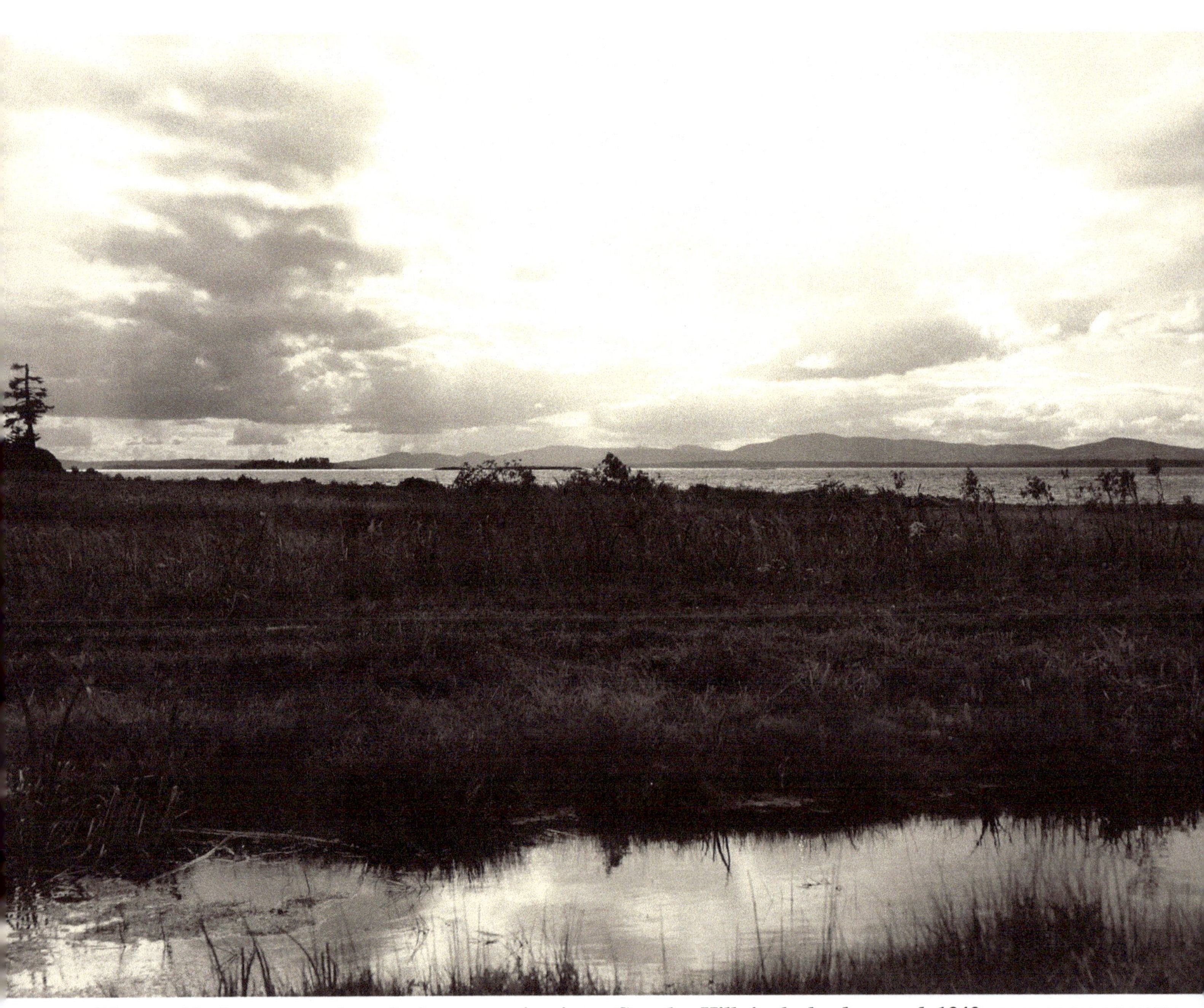

The pond in the swamp where the ice was cut in winter, Camden Hills in the background, 1940. GEOFFREY BAKER PHOTO

The Newspapers and the News

Jim's letters, even when short, would share some kind of news of his family or news of Penobscot Bay. He loved receiving news either of the summer family or the outside world. His letters reflect that he kept up to date with current events by reading the newspapers and listening to the radio. My father sent him subscriptions, for many years, to a Boston newspaper and later to the *Maine Coast Fisherman*. The newspapers, especially, played an important role in his life, as they were considered to be a prime source of his learning to read and write, as explained earlier.

Jim expressed his great appreciation for receiving subscriptions to the newspapers. In a March 6, 1916, letter to my father he wrote, *"well wilcot i am getting the paper oll rite and i tell you i am interested in it i go to the mail every day for to get my paper and i am ever so much obligegt to you for it."* The following year, on February 25, 1917, he wrote, *"well wolcot i get the paper all rite and i am verry glad to have them this winter for that they are verry interesting."*

On February 23, 1920, Jim wrote: *"well wolcot in regards to the clipens you sent me out of the papers i see oll that cind of neuse for i take the daly paper and when i get to the mail i get a hole armlod at a time."*

On December 10, 1928, Jim wrote:

in ancer to yours of nov 26 wich i receved some time ago and olso the maine cost paper wich i am verry interested in and i have Bin having it now for 3 years and i am so sorrow i dident rite you Before But i am still on the island and didnt have eny pen so i thought i Better get Bissey with a pensel so please excuse pensel riting   well wolcott i thank you verry verry much for the thats [thoughts] of me to send me the Maine cost fisherman wich i have Bin taking. . . . so will close for this time and thank you again for thinking of me with that wonderfull papper   But i have it cummin to me regler every month

When writing to Wolcott, Jim liked to include news of the island communities of the Bay, as well as news of events and people of neighboring islands. In an early letter of November 14, 1915, Jim wrote:

well wilket i sopes you herd about the in of dark harber burnen down it burnet down the same weak you left   it made a hote fire for a little wile it was just 2 ours from the time the fire started and it was all Burnt flat to the ground

Jim's letters contain frequent mention of Great Spruce Head, Bear Island's closest neighboring island, linked by a sandbar at very low tides. In a January 1920 letter, Jim wrote,

well wilcott mr porter has sold the tramp the seckend that is his yoat and is agoing tow fix the hipacanpas [Hippocampus] over and he has got oll throu with capten green so he will have a new capten next summer

In a May 23, 1927, letter he noted:

*well wilcot one of the porter Boys has Bin down to the island a
little wile this spring he had coppel of his frends with him it was
fearfeld [Fairfield] that was down i went to dark harbor and
met them and landed them at great spruce head but the feller
lives there took them away . well they have a new capten on spruce
head this year again*

Eagle Island, where Mrs. Andrews stayed in the summer of
1904, a visit that led to her purchase of Bear, is another close neigh-
bor. Eagle Island's year-round residents outnumbered those of Bear
and Great Spruce Head, and the Quinn family predominated.

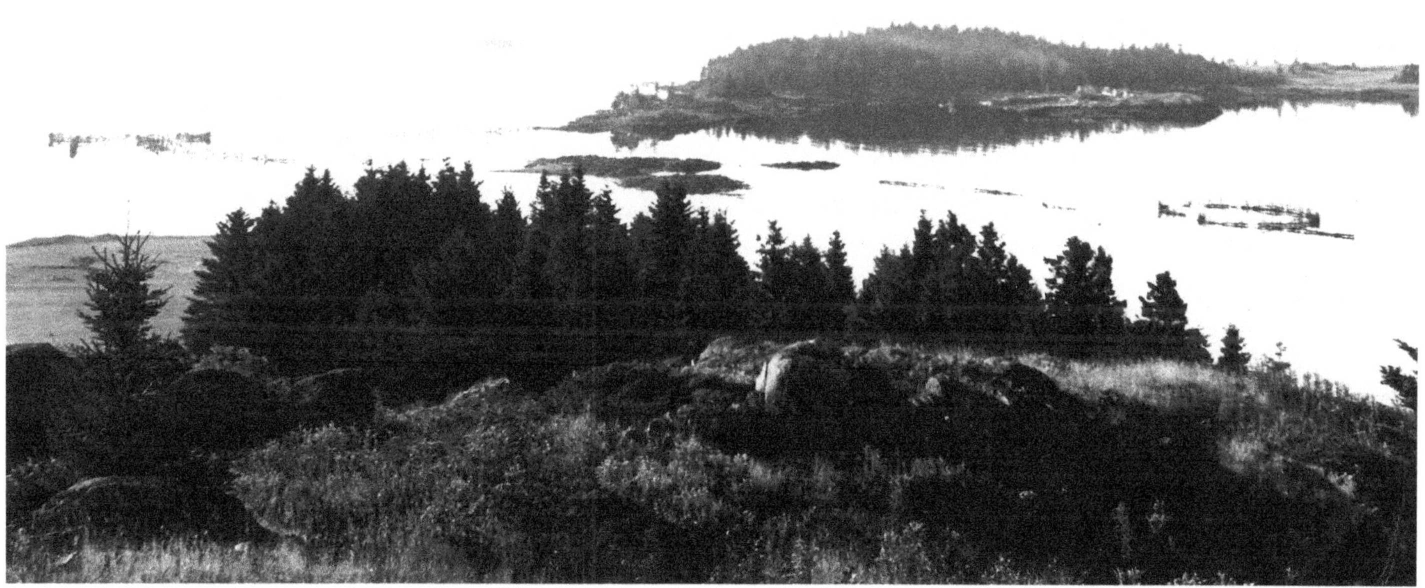

**Looking at Bear Island from Great Spruce Head Island, showing the ledges and herring weirs between the islands,
1940.** GEOFFREY BAKER PHOTO

On June 11, 1917, Jim wrote:
well wolcott did you here that aBout John quin of eagel island
Beying ded   he died a few weeks ago and also you no rodney eaton
on little Dear island   the Boat Builder he got drouned last weak

On April 13, 1919, he commented, *"eager quin has Bin very*
sick this winter and now is in the hospital at rockland   he has Bin
oprated on But is getting beter now."

Jim's letter of May 23, 1927, included some building news:
well wolcott they are Bilding a new cottage on eagel this year   it is
sawers that is having it Bilt   it is to Be a Brick house and had a well
drilled on there   they had to go over 400 feat to get water enough

Jim's news of the Bay included references to the mail carrier of
the US Mail Service, an important person in the lives of the island
people and their steady contact with the outside world. The mail
was delivered from Sunset on Deer Isle to Eagle Island. As Jim
wrote on February 23, 1920:
well wolcott you hasked me if i got the sugar from Mrs hall   i
did   i receved it oll rite and i think it is very cind of her sending
it to me   i come verry near not getting it for the mail man fell
in the reach thrue the ice and the sugar got a little wet But it did
not hurt it eanny

A later letter of December 29, 1934, mentioned Earl Howard:
well wolcot you remBer earl howard the mail carrier he was
taking verry ill and was taking to Bangor hostuol and was thrue
2 oprashens and the last we herd was doing well and his yungest
sun is carren the mail

The history of the mail carriers of Penobscot Bay is also the history of the mail boats. The primary service of the mail carrier was that of delivery and pickup of mail. However, the boats also served to carry passengers to and from the islands. These would be people who lived on the islands, or vacationed there, and did not have their own boats to get around. Today, the mail boat still runs from Eagle Island to the other offshore islands, still carries passengers and makes special trips, and the Quinn family still ably manages the service.

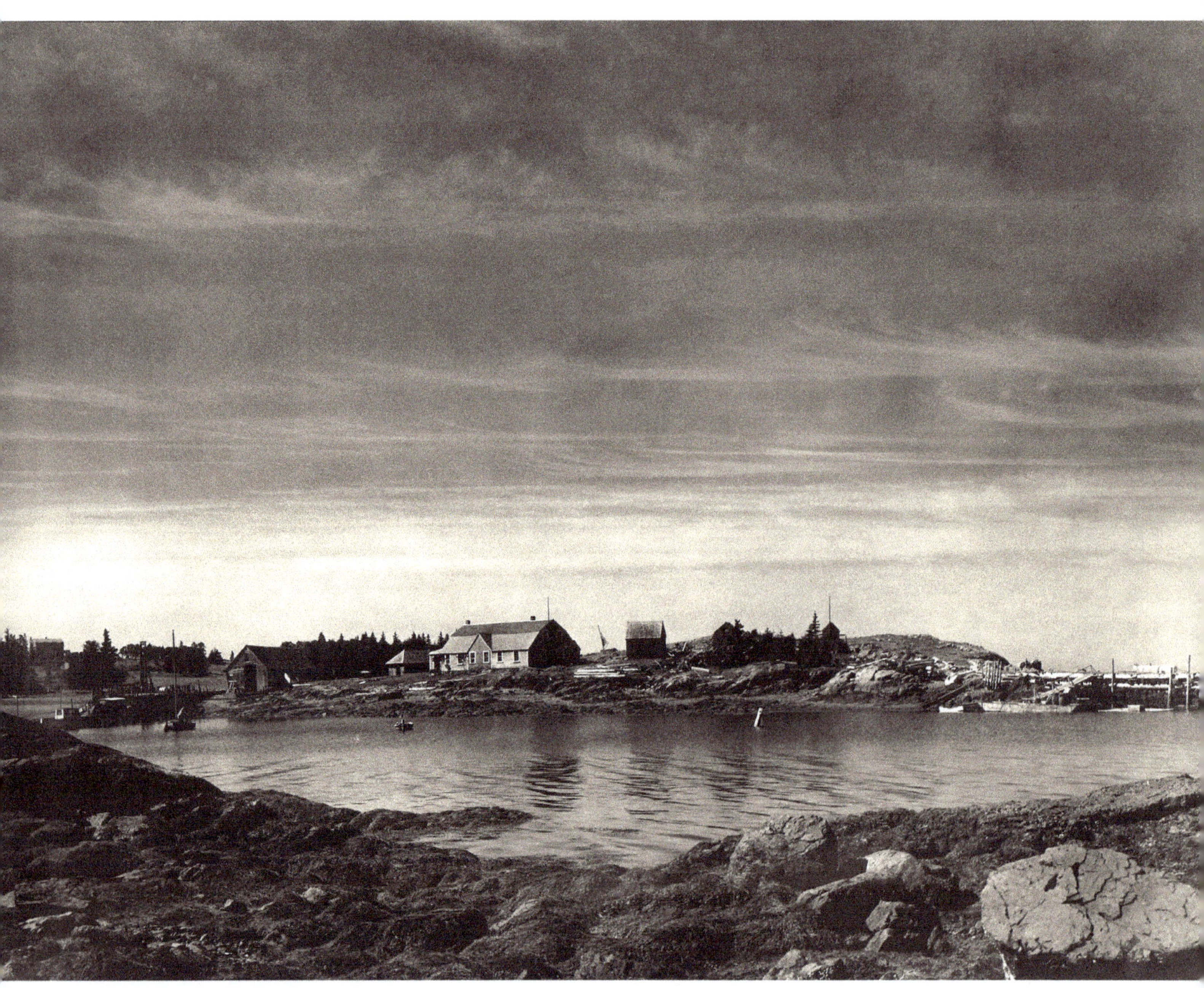

The Harbor: Harbor House, the wharves, and Hardie Head at low tide, from Camp Point (Piggie's Point), 1940.
GEOFFREY BAKER PHOTO

Reporting on the Weather

Most of the letters contain some mention of the weather. Those written in the wintertime would often relate dramatic tales of the Penobscot Bay freezing over, strong winds, and zero-degree temperatures. Jim had a strong dislike for the cold and anything to do with ice, especially an iced-over bay or harbor. In an early letter of the collection, February 25, 1917, Jim recalled: *"this has been a offel cold winter here i have Bin frose up that u cood not get of the island for ice it was ice from Bear island to little spros."*

Some winters appear to have been worse than others. On January 20, 1918, Jim wrote to Mrs. Fuller: *"terrebel winter here i am all surounnd with ice if it dont change soon it will have the hole bay froze up."*

On March 24,1918, he recounted:
Wel wilcet my big Boat got badly heart in the ice this winter she was laying to the out side of the warf and the ice Jamed her so bad thar she Brok some of her timbers and 2 of her planking i have got her fixed now i had to poot 7 new tinkers in her and 2 new plank i done it myself

In his February 23, 1920, letter he reported:
and i dont get of the island verry often to get the mail for oll i
can yuse is a row Boat and the ice Bothers ofly some days we cant
see eanny water for ice and some days there eant much and thems
the times i go to the mail

In a letter to "Frends Mrs King and mrs fuller," dated March 4, 1923, Jim wrote:
the hole Bay is frozen up but can see water as far as chanel rock
an flin island. . . . But yet cood walk from Bear island to weBsters
head north haven i have the ospray laying to the morn [mooring]
in the harBer now in the ice i come verry near to losing her this
winter i had her over to sproos hed had her fasand to 2 of mr
porters morns and the ice shifted and took the Boat and 2 morns
down to the loar Beach at peapoint and mr sheperd got a Bord of
her and got herser and tied the end of it to a trea on shore and
held her unti i got a Bord of her and i got her out of that Jam of
ice and got her over to the Bar and we had to get the ice saws and
saw a chanel into the harBer and got her in safly

Harsh winters were also cold winters. On January 28, 1924, Jim wrote Wolcott about a "cold snap" of 26 degrees Fahrenheit below zero that by the following day had risen to minus 18 degrees:
you no that is offel cold for here for the tempther dont drop here
like it dos on the main the salt are don't let it drop like it wood
ware it is dry cold yestday the veper was thick like fog that i
counot see the other end of the island . . . but it isent going to
stand long this way for the glass is going up for a sudden change

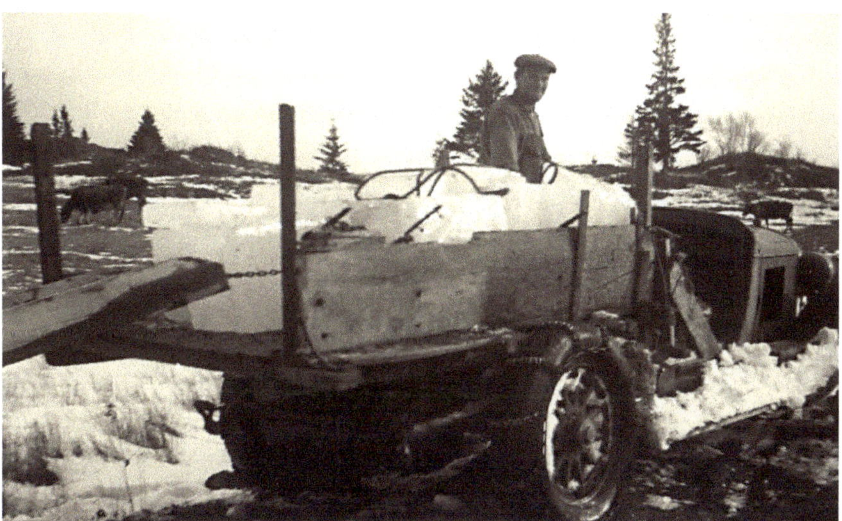

Hauling ice in the winter for keeping in the icehouse, 1939.
BEAR ISLAND FAMILY ARCHIVES

Reading the direction of air pressure in the "glass" on a barometer instrument was and is to this day a time-honored predictor of weather, not dependent on electricity or satellite information. "Going up" means greater air pressure and improving atmospheric conditions.

Not all winter weather was temperature related. On May 24, 1928, Jim told of

one of the worst storms this winter that i have see ever since i lived on the island and it come rite on the hy run of tides and it wasnt safe to go on the warf for you cood not stand up and the tide sweep rite across the see wall from the Boat house to the woods i tell you it looked Bad for a wile

Ice often meant isolation. Jim wrote Wolcott Fuller on February 9, 1934:

*well wolcott this sure is a tuff winter here   the Bay is frozen up
our Boats frose in the harBor we can walk to little spruse and to
mark island down to weBsters hed and crab trea point noth
haven i am witing thse few lines But don't know when i will get
to the post office wether offel cold trempther 12 belo zero this
morning i poot up ice last weak had 20 inch thick*

Jim continued to write in the same letter:
*dear frend Just a few lins more this feb 11 havent got to post
office yet and dont kon how long it will Be Before i get there there
is so much ice it isent safe to walk and cant get a boat out*

The letter went on to describe more icy conditions:
*the ice Braker Boat named KickaBe [Kickapoo] is having quit a
Job braking ice in ponoscott Bay this winter   feb 16 still ice
Bound But Bony quin got to spruce hed last night and is going to
eagel today and i am agoing to try and give him this letter to
may so will close   best regards from oll to oll*

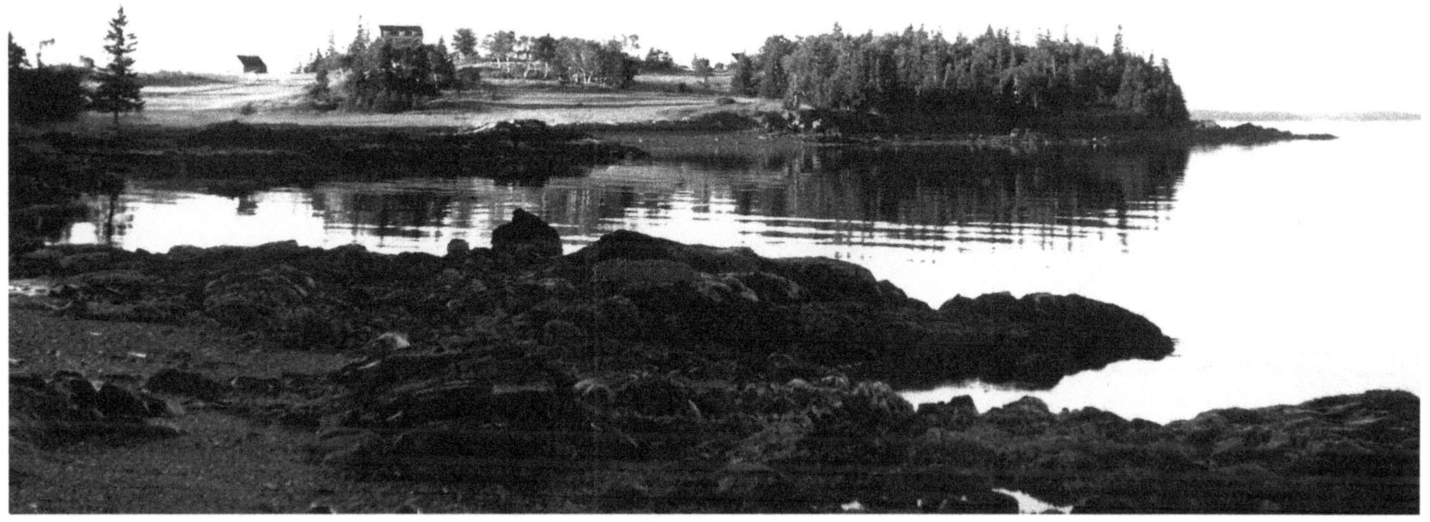

View of Bear Island looking south, with fields, Hay Barn, and roof of Big House in the distance, 1940.
GEOFFREY BAKER PHOTO

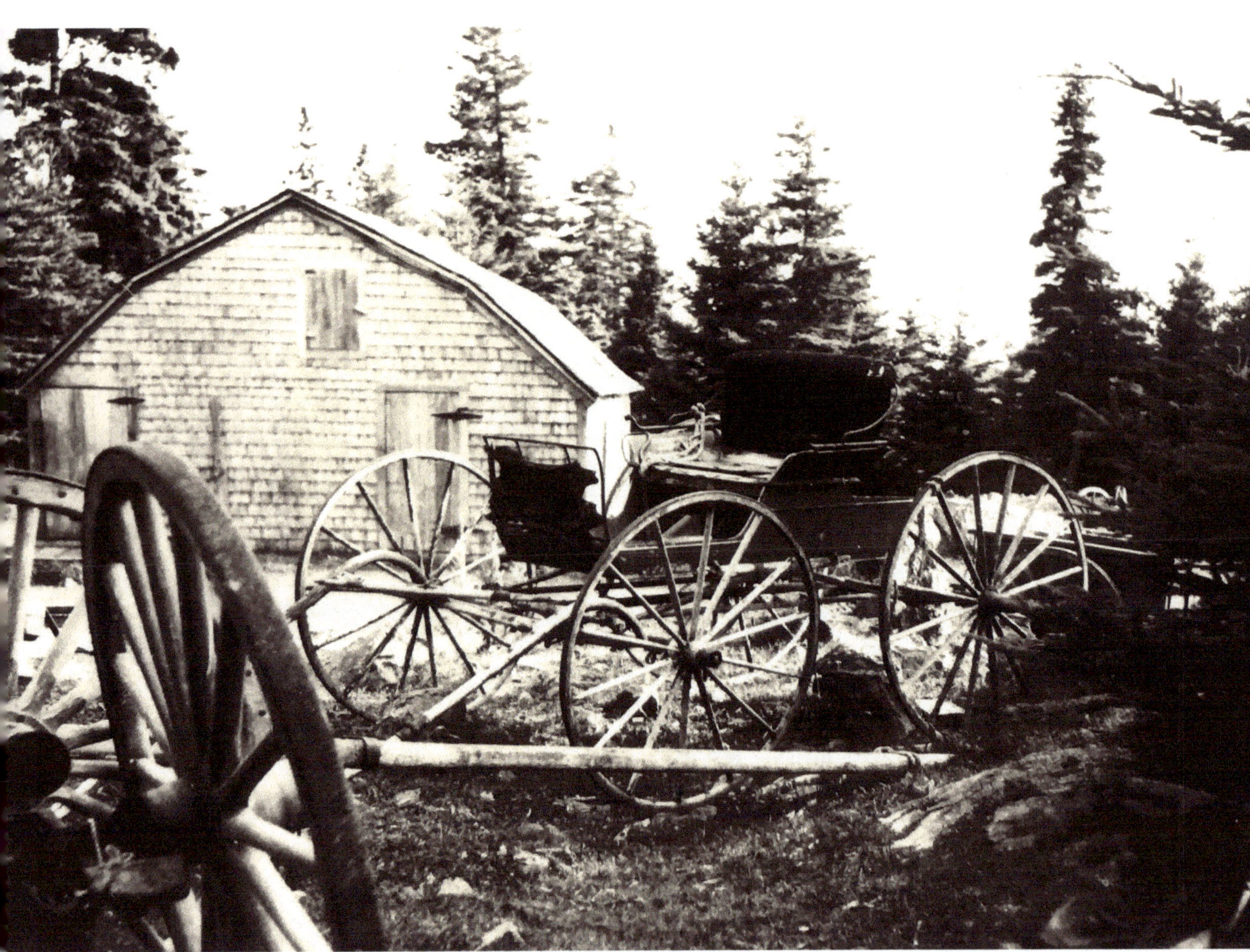

Four-wheel horse-drawn carriage and wagon wheels, 1939. BEAR ISLAND FAMILY ARCHIVES

Farming the Island

The sea and the land were the primary sources of food for the Hardie family. A great deal of time and energy were devoted to farming the island in season and using what was produced for family consumption. All members of the family participated in the multiple farming duties.

There were livestock on the island, both for work and food, and they needed to be taken care of. Oxen were kept to haul wagons loaded with wood, hay, and stones. Jim later acquired a used Ford sedan, which he converted into a truck for hauling loads such as stone and lumber. Cows were kept for the milk; pigs and chickens for eating, including the eggs from the chickens. Sheep provided mutton to eat, as well as wool. Sheep were kept on the island and pastured on nearby Compass Island in the summertime. Enough wool was produced from the shearing of the sheep to take the fleece to the woolen mill in Camden. As mentioned earlier, Alice Hardie milked the cows and used the wool from the sheep to knit clothing for the family.

Wild animals and birds were hunted for food. Jim wrote on February 9, 1934, that *"wolcott goes guning once and a wile to pass*

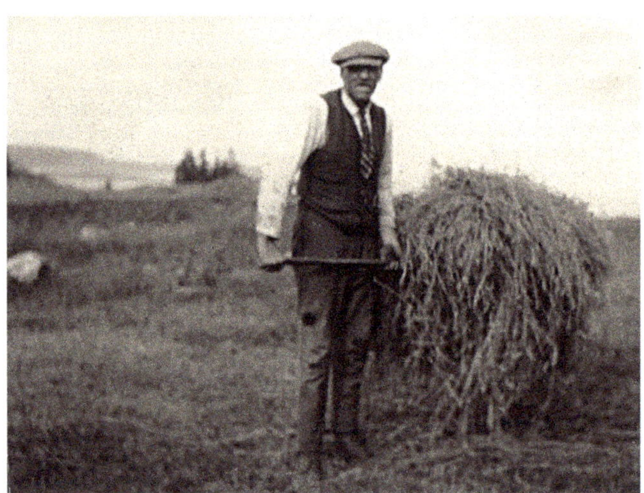

Jim haying by the Cook House (Eating House), 1926.
BEAR ISLAND FAMILY ARCHIVES

time away he got 2 wisslers (ducks) yestday and he got 2 today   we ar agoing to have them backed for dinner sunday." Besides duck, Jim and his boys shot other large sea birds for food.

Jim's affection for living things extended to many of the animals he kept. The letters contain ample reference to them. Jim gave them names, and he talks sadly of their passing. A letter of February 4, 1916, mentioned:

i hav not got Billy the ox now i have a nother one he eant so big as Billy was he is nise and quite ox But he is not verry strong But i ges i will get along with him you no the little Bool i had on little sprous head i had to sell to him for he was oll aparents of Being ugly i Brot him on Bear island and i tell you he looked pretty ugly so i thought i Better sell him

He wrote to Wolcott on January 3, 1917, *"i cild my pig decem-ber 27 and december 28 i cild my black calf and i wish you cood of bin here to help me."* Jim later described, in a January 12, 1919, letter, taking care of another bull: *"i kiled my ugly Bull a weak ago and he was offel ugly."* In an early picture in the family albums, "Bessie the calf" is named.

Of the pets, Jim talks of one dog in particular, Jack. He was not only a pet but a hunter. In a January 1920 letter, Jim wrote: *"well wilcott i did not do eanny gunning this fall for i have Ben tow Bissy but Jack has got me one more mink."* Jim lamented Jack's death in a November 19, 1925, letter:

> *well wilcott i have a offel nice dog now giving me By your mother*
> *he is a Butie now   he is growing fast   i had to shoot Jack it was a*
> *hard thing for me to do But he got very searrice sick and there*
> *was no chance for him to get well so i poot him out of his suffren*

Jim and the Hardies' farming work on Bear carried on a practice set up in the nineteenth century. Fields and open spaces abounded on Bear when Mrs. Andrews purchased the island. Like most

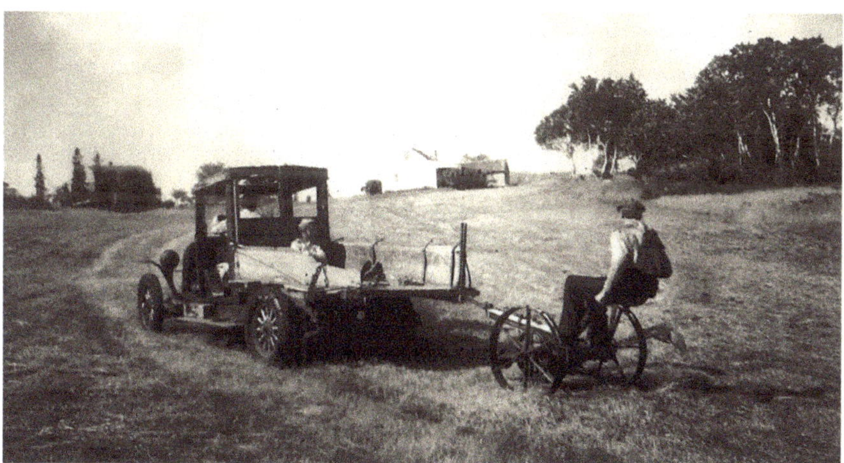

Mowing hay below the Cook House (Eating House), 1939.
BEAR ISLAND FAMILY ARCHIVES

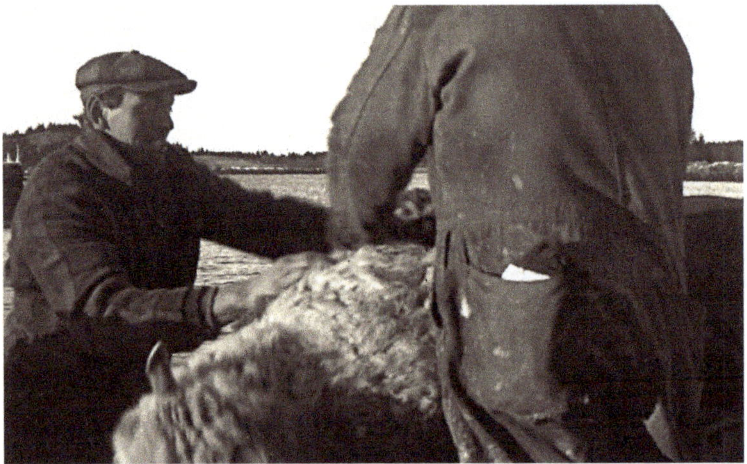

Jim and son shearing sheep, 1943. BEAR ISLAND FAMILY ARCHIVES

islands in the Bay, the island had been extensively cleared of trees and farmed in the nineteenth century. The forests had been cut down as well, to sell for firewood for the lime kilns on the mainland in Rockport and Rockland.

Jim hayed the open fields to produce fodder for the animals. The hay was stored in the Hay Barn located on the high ridge of the open fields in the center of the island. The livestock were housed in another barn, closer to the harbor area. Jim used an existing clearing in the northern forest area near the barn for his garden.

The family grew a variety of vegetables, including turnips, carrots, beets, and squash. Wolcott Hardie and Winslow Hardie both relate that Alice Hardie would can vegetables as well as store them in the cellar or second-floor area of the Harbor House. There was a natural spring, or water hole, nearby for water for both the animals and use in the garden. The water hole is still known as the "cow's well."

On the edge of the clearing is evidence of one of the old cellar holes that were on the island when it was purchased in 1904.

According to Wolcott Hardie, there were eleven old cellar holes of earlier nineteenth-century houses. Jim and the boys would dig out the rock from the holes to use to build the roads and the base for the tennis court started in the 1930s.[36]

Jim planted potatoes that provided a significant source of food for the family. There is an area in the middle of the island still known today as Jim's potato patch. From his early days as a foster child on Prince Edward Island, working in potato fields, Jim must have learned not only how to plant and grow potatoes but also how to store them, and most importantly, he must have learned that they were a dependable year-round source of food.

There were apple trees for fruit, some of which were probably planted on the island during the nineteenth century and some planted by Jim. A dozen or more of the apple trees still produce today; some are good for cooking, and some are good for eating.

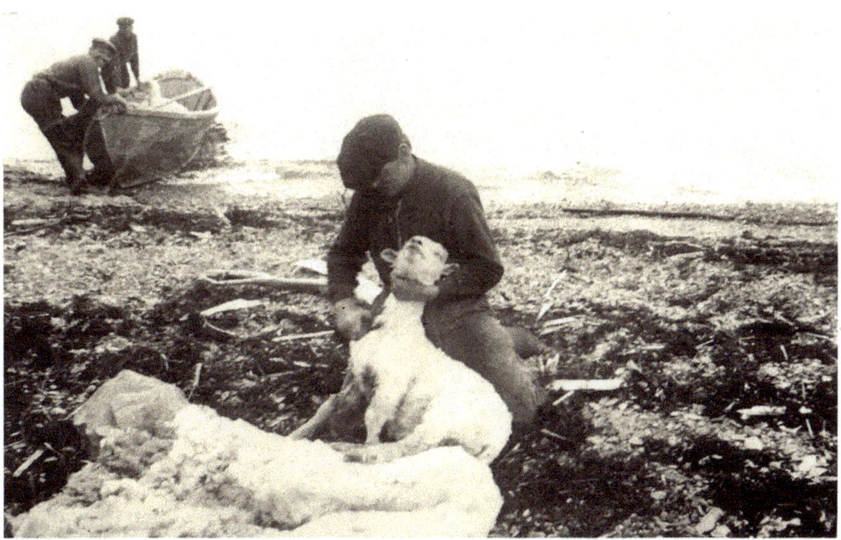

Shearing sheep and loading them in a dory for trip to Compass Island for the summer, 1943. BEAR ISLAND FAMILY ARCHIVES

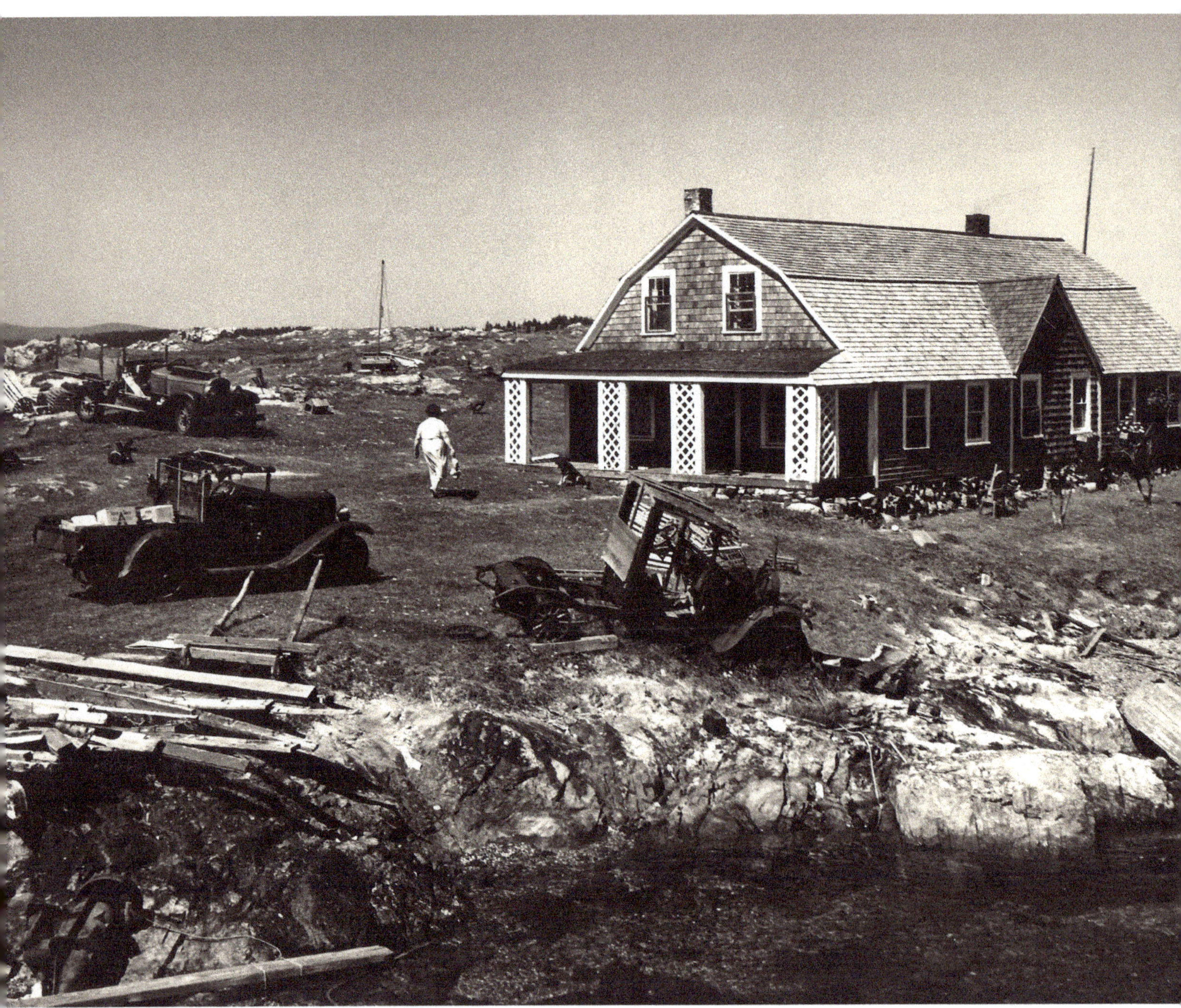

Harbor House and three vehicles, 1940. GEOFFREY BAKER PHOTO

Dealing with Medical Emergencies

A question that arises for anyone living on an island is how to deal
with sicknesses and emergencies. Jim's letters cover accidents on
land and sea as well as sicknesses. All are harrowing events for their
isolation from medical help. One incident involved Jim's son James,
who, startled from sleep in the boat cabin, fell and cut himself badly.
On November 14, 1915, Jim writes:

> *well wilket did you here that my son James come verry nere geten*
> *kild i will tell you just how it hapend we was up to little Dear*
> *island one sunday and we was comen home in the eaven and*
> *James went to sleat in the caben and we was all out in the cockpit*
> *we got down to the end of the chainlinks and we herd a noise in*
> *the caben and there was the pore little feller stretched out on the*
> *caben flore where he had fell agast the Knox engine fly weal and*
> *it struck him over the rite eie and it gave him a nofel cut s so i*
> *turned my boat and put to the Doctors and he had to have 4 stchs*
> *put in and i cood not put him a sleet so he had to suffer oll the*
> *pain But he is oll well now*

The end of World War I brought sickness worldwide. Jim reports in a letter of January 12, 1919:

> *well wolcot every thing is Just the same as when you left But we have had a prettie Bad fall   for we had oll the influenza and had it hard and you remember herBert he died with it   But we are oll well now*

At that time of the Spanish Flu, or the Great Influenza epidemic, the household was composed of Jim, Alice, Lillian, James, and Wolcott. The children would have been eight, six, and five years old. One wonders what remedies and medicines they might have used for an entire household to survive a pandemic!

A highly unusual incident, requiring Jim's quick and knowledgeable thinking, took place aboard the *Wego* in the summer of 1931, when Jim took Aunt Lucy King out for an afternoon cruise on the Bay. While sitting on the boat, apparently Aunt Lucy suddenly died. Jim knew that a person of authority would be needed to sign a death certificate, so he flagged down a steamboat heading for Islesboro, knowing that the captain could sign a certificate. The body was transferred to the steamboat, which went to Rockland. There arrangements were made with one of her daughters to accompany the deceased by train to Chicago.[37]

Jim was well aware of the need to plan for medical and health emergencies that would require a trip to the mainland for help. In a February 24, 1935, letter Jim writes about

> *some very tuff winter wether it ceaps the harBor fool of ice about oll the time   i ceap my Boat over Back the island where the wear is i can use her from there when i cant get out the harBor in case of mergeseng*

Another major health incident that Jim describes is his own illness, in a May 10, 1937, letter.

Dear frend wolcott: …we are all well at island except my self and i am having offel hard luck now   now i will tell you   march 31 rite in the Best of my scloping i was close to the Bank prying logs with a crobar to get it up so i could saw it for wood and my bar sliped and i fell over the Bank in a rock pile but got out with Just a sprant ankle   but that laid me up for 2 weaks for 1 weak i couldent poot my foot to the floor   well i Just got so i could work good so last friday march 7 (sic) i went over to sunset to bring the children home for weak end and i went to step from the warf out to my boat and my foot sliped and fell against my hous hurting my side so i Brot my family home and i got home i couldent set down or lay down so next morning the Boys too me to casten to the doctor   he poot me thrue exray and found i had Broke a rik so he

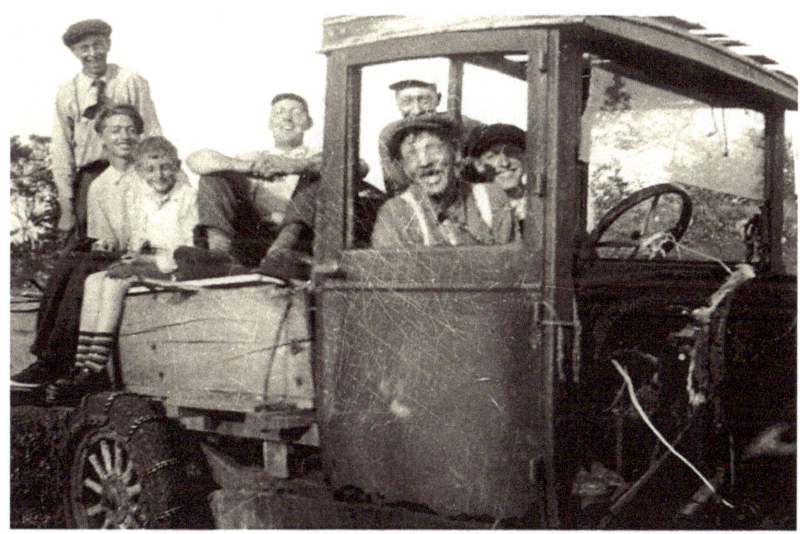

Jim, five sons, and Walter Shepard in working vehicle, 1943.
BEAR ISLAND FAMILY ARCHIVES

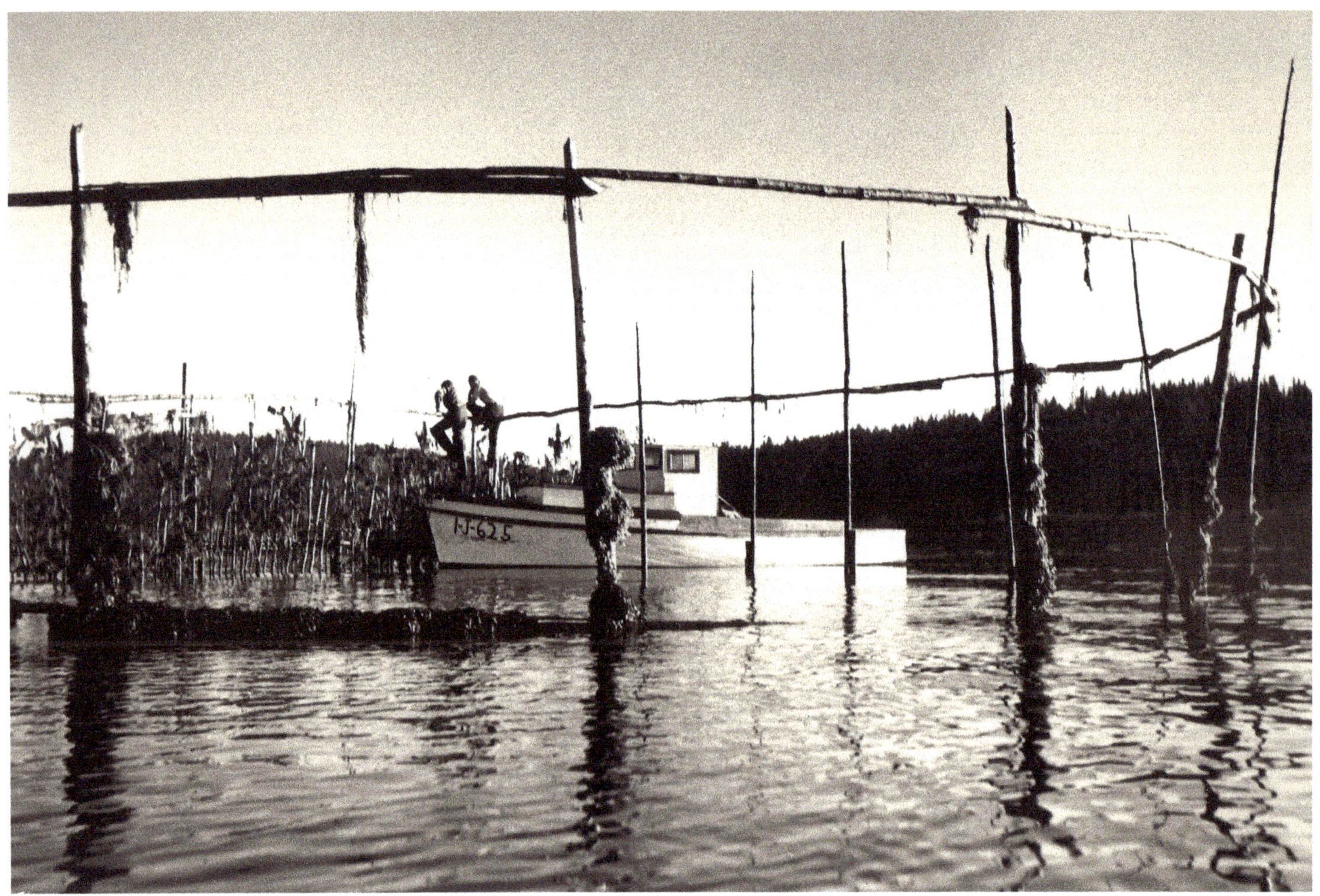

Herring weir constructed with alder poles, 1940. GEOFFREY BAKER PHOTO

*plastered me up and told me not to do a thing for 3 weaks and i
have to see him again in a few days But it is offel thing for me to
lay up for 3 weaks   But the way i feal i am glad to …. so will
Bring this to close for this and i get out to work again   i am in
Bed riting this letter   very truly yours James Hardie*

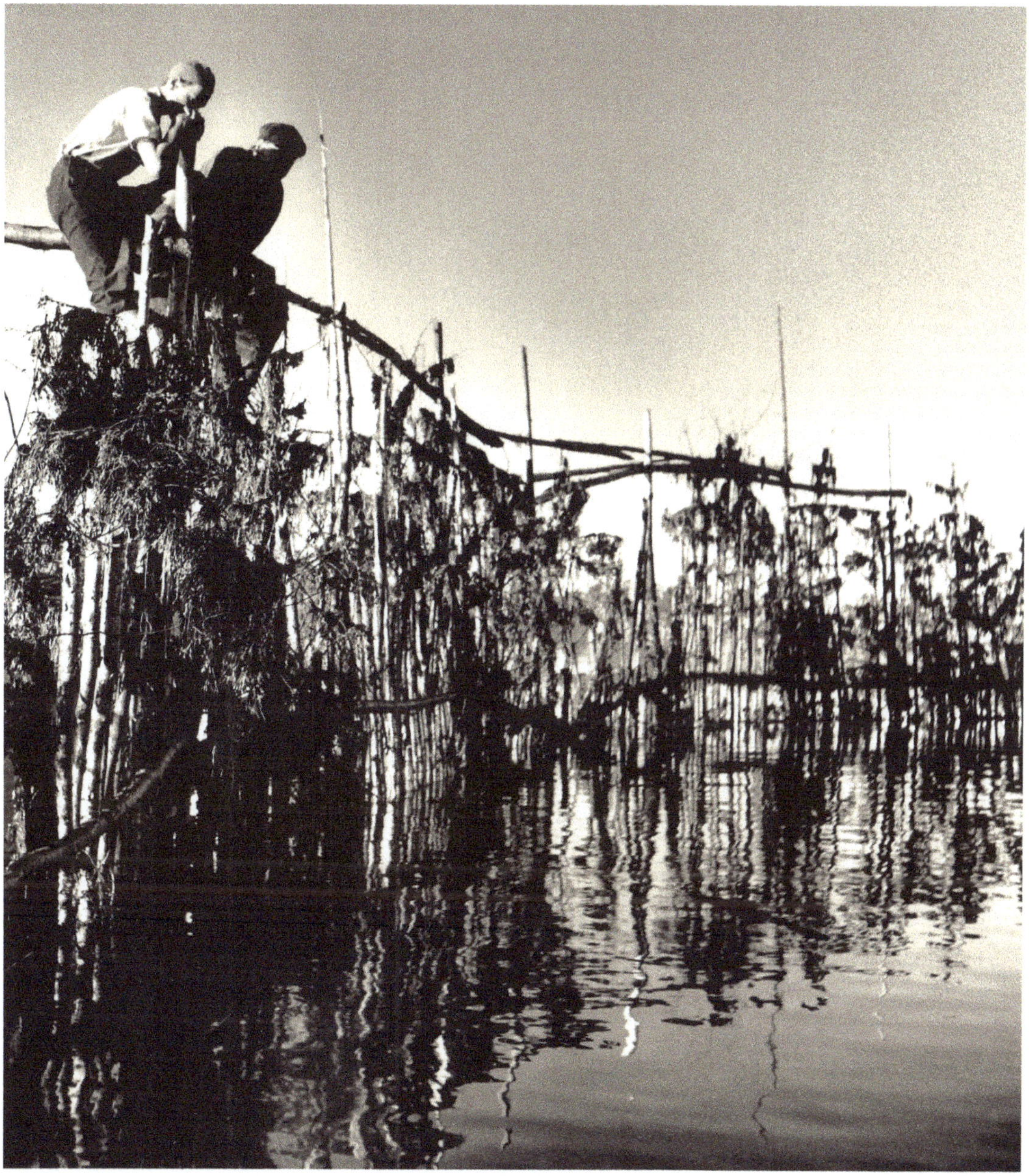

Overlooking the weir, 1940.   GEOFFREY BAKER PHOTO

By coincidence, this May 10, 1937, letter was the last in my father's collection from Jim until 1953.

For people who made their living on the sea, accidents related to boat use were not uncommon and were often serious. Winslow Hardie, Jim's third son, barely escaped death in 1943 when the gas tanks exploded and the boat caught fire off of Mark Island while coming home. Winslow was forced to go into the water, clinging to a life preserver. The explosion was seen from Stonington and by the lighthouse keeper on Mark Island, and boats were sent to the scene. Winslow was rescued from the water "nearly exhausted from his struggle with the heavy sea that was running at the time, and thoroughly chilled by the icy water."[38]

Jim himself suffered the loss of his front teeth from an accident on his boat. In Winslow's tape recording, he talks about how the boys grew up with their father taking apart and fixing boat engines, switching and interchanging parts. Winslow related that one day Jim was trying to start an engine, by spinning the flywheel by hand, when the flywheel spun off, hit Jim, and that was how Jim lost his two front teeth.[39] Curiously enough, I never noticed that Jim had lost his front teeth, probably because he always sported a mustache. Nor did I hear people speak of this, nor did Jim mention it in any letters. However, it is evident in pictures, especially ones of Jim smiling happily.

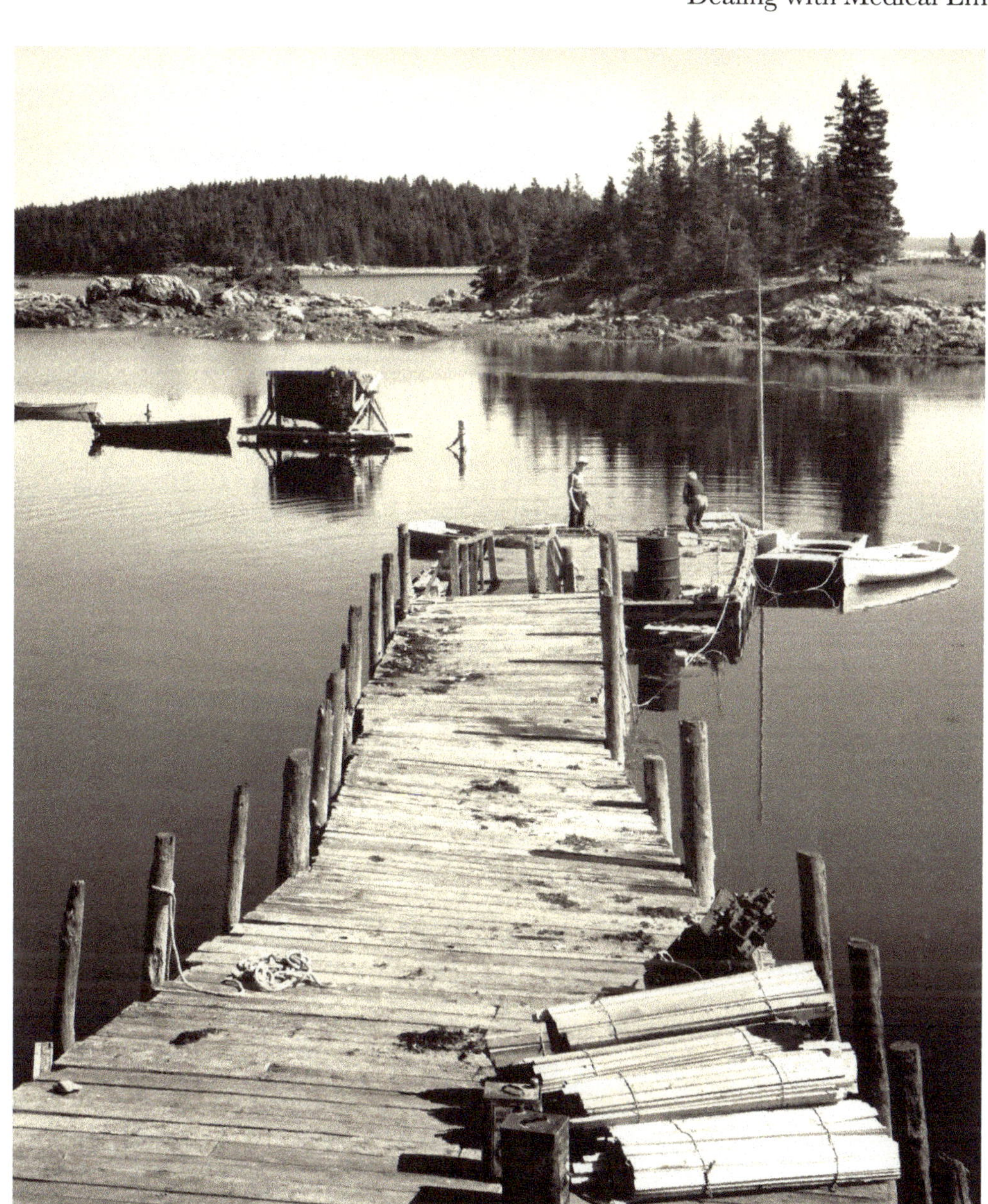

Inner Harbor wharf and dock, with view toward Camp Point (Piggie's Point) and Great Spruce Head Island, 1940. GEOFFREY BAKER PHOTO

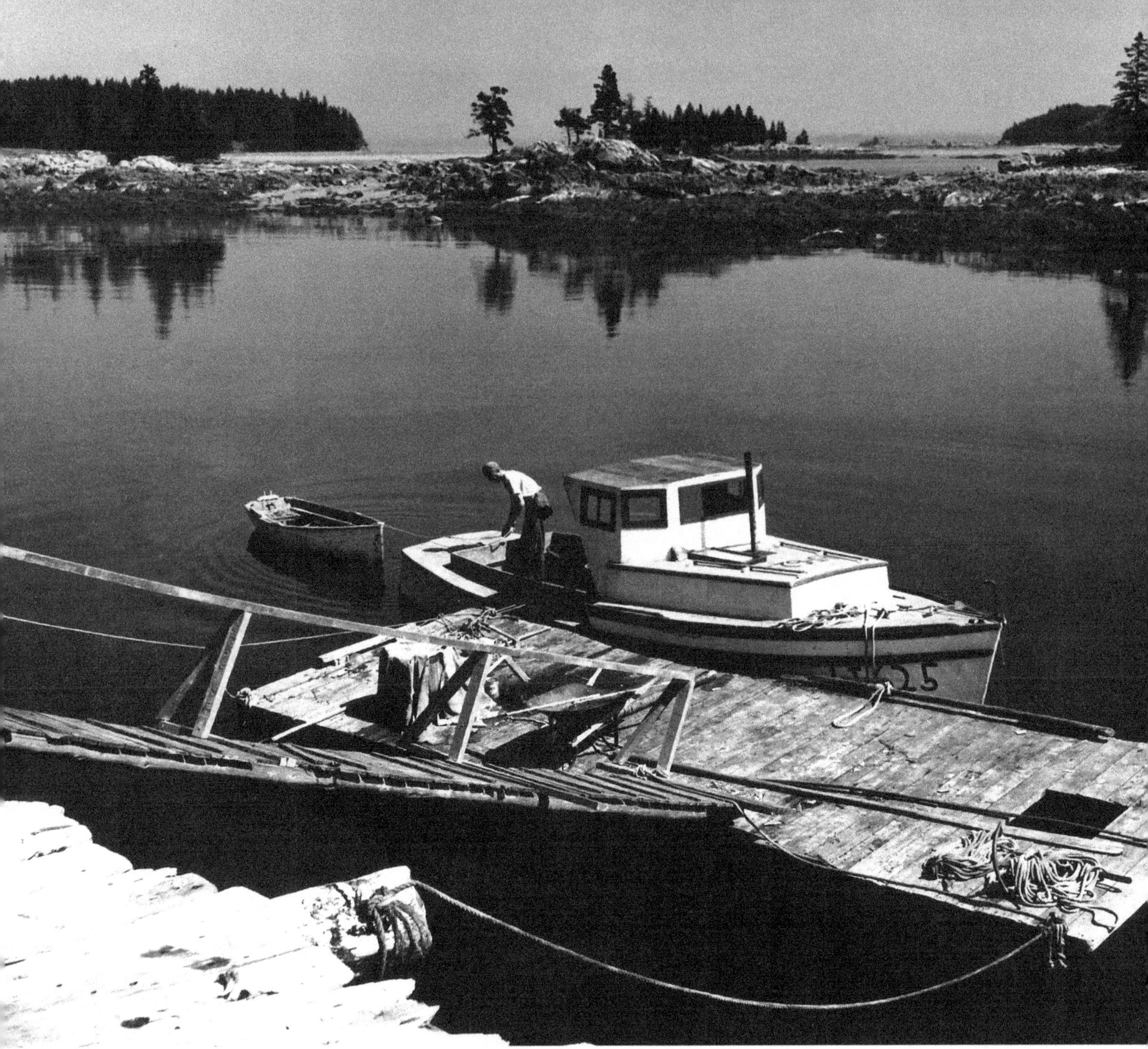

Outer wharf with float, with view toward Camp Point (Piggie's Point) and Great Spruce Head Island, 1940.
GEOFFREY BAKER PHOTO

Hard Times

A constant theme in Jim's letters is that of making ends meet and keeping the family fed. Precise information on the amounts from the different sources of income or the total thereof is not available in Jim's case, but like many independent fishermen and islanders, he combined several sources to face that challenge. It appears that Jim received a regular monthly salary as caretaker from the owners of Bear Island. Caroline Wolcott Andrews's two daughters shared the monthly payments equally between their families. There were bonus gifts at the end of the year.

There was additional compensation, also shared equally, for extra activities from which all owners benefitted, such as house repairs, road building, gardening, or constructing the tennis court. Work and jobs carried out by personal request from a member of the family, such as fixing or building a boat, brought in additional compensation for Jim or a member of his family, especially during the summer months when the owners and their families were in residence. The Hardies were compensated for supplying chickens, eggs, milk, and vegetables from their garden. Alice Hardie and her sister Josie were paid for doing laundry. Josie cooked for the summer family. Wolcott and Winslow Hardie provided lobsters, clams, and fish. The only documentation on this comes from a handwritten itemized list kept by one branch of the family and sent to the other branch of the family about who paid what to whom for the years 1933–1937.

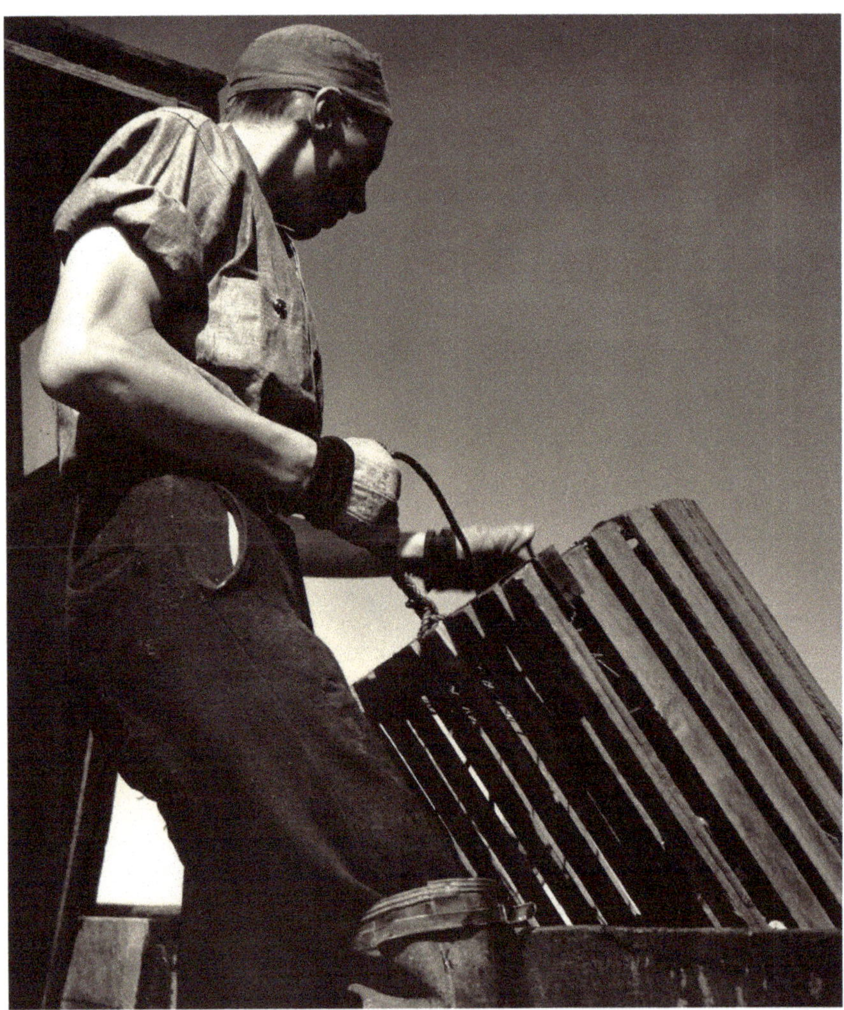

Pulling in a lobster trap, 1940. GEOFFREY BAKER PHOTO

Although it is not specified anywhere, one can assume that Jim and his family lived in the Harbor House as part of his caretaking arrangement. That was still the practice for caretakers on Bear Island into the decade of the 1970s. Additionally, the harbor served as a base of operations to keep the boats and fishing equipment for Jim and his sons to carry out their fishing occupations. Jim and his

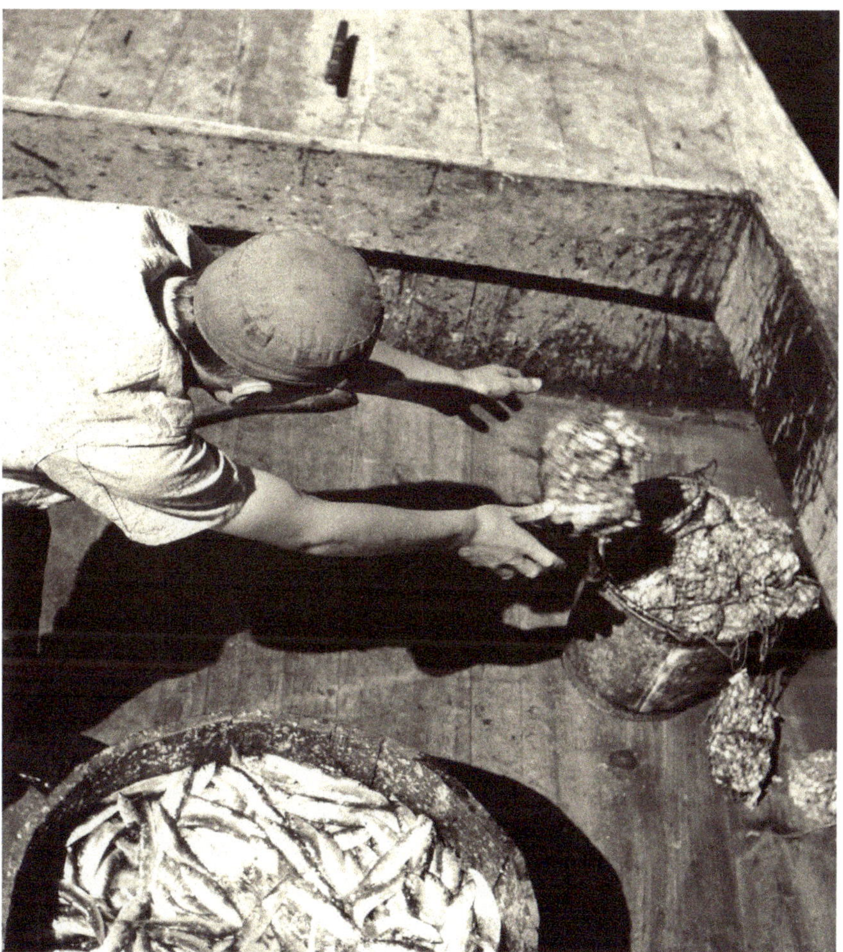

Bagging bait with herring to put in the lobster traps, 1940.
GEOFFREY BAKER PHOTO

sons sold fish, clams, scallops, and lobsters on the mainland and Deer Isle. What all this added up to for the Hardie family on an annual basis is not known, but from Jim's letters he indicates that meeting the financial needs of the family was a concern that seemed to increase as the family grew and times became harder during the Great Depression of the 1930s and wartime of the 1940s.

Even before then, Jim writes on February 25, 1917: *"i tell you wolcott times geting pritty hart in some places we cant By eanny pettoes here or eanny sugar so i dont no what we are agon to do if it ceaps on."* On June 11, 1917, during World War I, he writes, *"i have Been verry Busy where the times is so hard i have Ben away claming in my Boat."* In a March 24, 1918, letter he mentioned, *"there was quite a few things in the food line that we run out of but we puld thrue by good manegment."*

Jim supplemented his income by accepting work off Bear Island in off-season times. In a December 10, 1928, letter, he describes moving temporarily to Sunset on Deer Isle in December of 1927 and planning to do so again. He wrote, *"i hav a few jobs to do over there for the Dear island yacht cluB and expect to get thrue By erly spring and Back on the island agin."*

The Great Depression impacted life in Penobscot Bay and thus in the Hardie Family. Jim wrote on June 6, 1933: *"we are all well at present and had a nother Boy Born march 16 it is offel to have a adish-ing in the family those hard time But cant Be helped."* This last addition to the family was Pearl, Jim and Alice's youngest son. Jim writes on December 25, 1933:

> *well mrs. fuller i nover now what hard time was since i have Bin on Bear island until now   it sure is getting to Be a hard life to Bring up such a family   i am trying to sclope when a chance But they are very scarce and also the weather has Bin offel Bad this fall*

Jim continues on with the theme of economic survival in an October 22, 1934, letter:

Dear frend wolcott: Just a line in ance to yours of october 17 glad to here from you and glad to here that mr and mrs Daves got there all rite and i thank you verry much for check   it is sure verry nice how you peapel treted me this year   i apreashent verry much for it was looking pritty hard for me for i had gone Back so that i was verry near my limet   well wolcott fishing not verry much But did do a little this year   But for the last 4 year i did not get a sent out of it and went Bakwards

Hard times continued as Jim recounts in a December 29, 1934, letter to Wolcott Fuller:

and the next chance i get i am going to camden we have a few sclopes to take over   we don't get out very often now   i have 9 galons and Wolcott has 9 galons and i want to get 150 ($1.50) per galon and i want to get some grain and then some more grocess and then if the Bay freses over we can live thrue   i kild one of the cows for met this winter and also had a pig and kild him last weak so i have me cow left this winter Becose i didn't get much hay

In later years, Jim writes about further hardships dealing with gas and food rationing during World War II, which is covered in the next chapter.

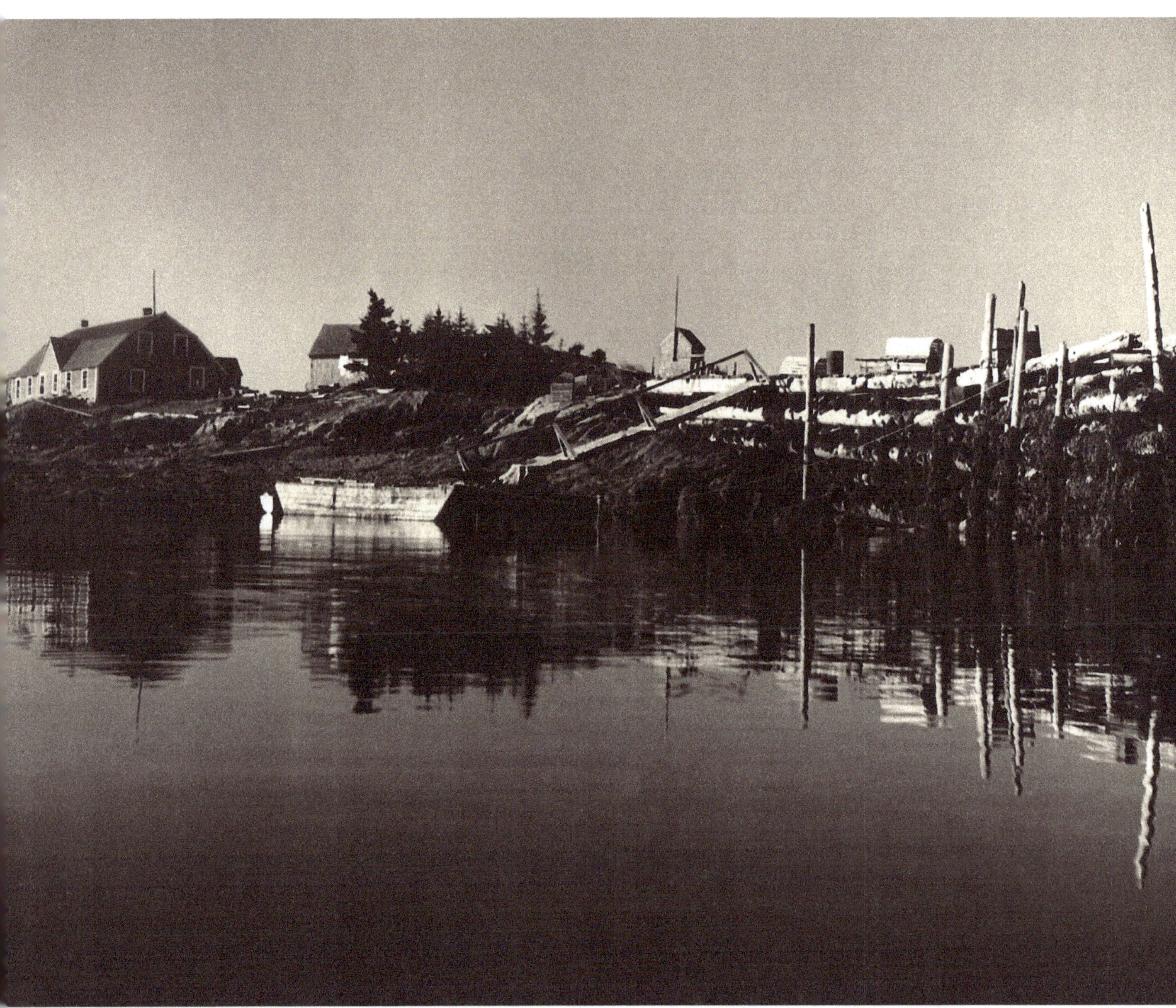

Outer wharf with float off of Hardie Head. When needed, the float could be used as a scow, 1940.
GEOFFREY BAKER PHOTO

Challenges and Transitions

During the decades of the 1930s and the early 1940s, changes took place on Bear Island. There were changes within the ownership of Bear among the heirs of Caroline Wolcott Andrews. These coincided with changes to Jim's relationship with her descendants as his employers and his role as caretaker. The summer of 1937 appears to have been a particularly challenging time for all concerned.

The transition had started at the beginning of the 1930s, when Lucy Andrews King died at the end of the summer. In January 1934, her sister, Caroline Andrews Fuller, died. Thus passed both daughters of the first owner, Mrs. Andrews. On February 9, 1934, Jim begins a letter to Wolcott Fuller, saying he is *very sorrow and surprised to here of your mother death i sure will miss her she has Bin a verry good frend to me.*

Caroline Fuller had been in failing health. Instead of summering on Bear Island, she rented a house on the mainland in Wiscasset from 1931 until 1933. During those years, her children visited Bear briefly or not at all.

Her death would change how Jim Hardie was compensated for his work on Bear Island. Prior to her death, it appears that the two daughters of Mrs. Andrews had the responsibilities for overseeing Jim's duties as caretaker and dealing with his compensation. Lucy Andrews King, the elder daughter, did this for her side of the family, and Caroline Andrews Fuller for her branch of the family. The two daughters apparently took on this role as Jim's employers at the outset of Jim's career as caretaker. It was a matriarchal situation from the beginning.

Caroline Wolcott Andrews, who bought the island in 1904, was a widow at the time, and she died in 1908. Lucy King was widowed in 1905. Caroline Fuller was herself widowed in 1910, the year Jim moved to Bear Island full time. When Lucy King died in 1931, apparently her two daughters, Ethel King DuMoulin and Marjorie King DuMoulin, who married brothers, and a son, John Andrews King, shared the responsibility as Jim's employers for their side of the family. Payments became irregular and the old ways proved unworkable.

In a December 25, 1933, letter to Caroline Fuller, Jim alludes to uneven forms of payment by the two families. He wrote: "*i don't hardly kno what i wood do if it wasent four you paying me regler for i only here from mr king a Bout 2 a year   i hadent herd from him since april 1 until 2 days ago mrs Dumolin payed the Bill.*"

On February 9, 1934, Jim writes to Wolcott: "*your mother had payed me up to DecemBer 1   i will enclose the last letter i recceved from her so as there will be no mis nder standing.*" It appears that by 1938, my father's sister, Rosy, took on the responsibilities as Jim's employer for her side of the family.

Starting in 1938, Rosy Fuller Kenison, my aunt, saved many letters from Jim, Alice Hardie, and members of her family, as well as other papers dealing with ownership among the heirs. These letters reflect troubles that Jim was having with the summer family, especially the King-DuMoulin side. John Andrews King, Lucy's son, known as Andy King, wanted to dismiss Jim immediately because of some incidents in the summer of 1937. According to the correspondence in Rosy's collection, problems with alcohol and an incident with a boat were attributed to Jim. Jim's letters in this collection are remarkable statements and assertions of his honor and sense of integrity. They are a self-defense and a plea to be treated as an equal human being.

On April 22, 1938, Jim wrote directly to Andy King:

i am now dropen you aline in regards to my esteshen wich proBly will not be verry interesten to you But never the less i cant Be helped   so now this is the sechuashen i have kno home only here on Bear island and i have payed my state taxes on evry thing i owe that is taxeBall even on my cattel and also down to my rowBoat for 27 years i have done this so this is all the home i have what money i made i spent here on the island to ceap my home up i have got kno money to By a home to poot my famly in so i will stay in my home on Bear island a wile longer and i am Bilden my wair now and Wolcott is agoing to stay on the island with me this summer so hopen you and family and frends may come to the island and enjoy the sumer and if eny thing i can do to help i wood be verry glad to do so i will do eny thing there is to Be don i am also fixe up the flower garden   i do that in rememBrs to your mother well wolcott and i have just Bilt a new boat and she is 36 ft long and we will lonch her next weak

Andy King's reply is unknown. Here in its entirety is Jim's even stronger response, dated May 12, 1938:

Dear Mr King in ancer to your letter receved sounds verry interesting after 27 years and 10 months and a half of servess

work as a capten and framer and carptner road builder and
evry thing you can nam even to a mancere   so Mr King there is
just 2 ways out of it   of corse your storry has gon iBrod to all
partes in oll famly   But i have sead nothing yet   But the way you
feal about it there has to be a lot sead yet   now Mr King the one
way is to forget and forgive   that way is O.K. with me   otherwise
as you say augist i will come to a point that it will be painful to
oll the famlys   i dont think there is eny nead of that   But of corse
if matters comes from bad to worce it will have to Be don   of corse
Mr King we cant expect to go thrue our hole life without pain
But trustng we can settel this matter in a decent way   now Mr
King if i remember rite one time last sumer you sed you had
ritten to the fullers saying that i had lived on the island so long
that i was out of my hed   But one thing i can thank god for i had
head enof to nok of drinking that i can prove to you in time   now
Mr King in regards to the offer you gave my son wolcott in the
letter you rote him   he told me he rote you that he wasnt intrested
in the job he sed you wanted him to furnish takels and all equrp-
ment and help for lauchen   he thought that was out of reason
and i realy did eagrea with him there   so i am holden this letter
to sho athorets what a wonderful offer you made one of my Boys
now here is the sichuishen   wolcott and i will get your boats and
evrthing redey for you on the time you stated and he will run the
boat for your famly for $25 per weak   if i am on the island and
my name is around here is verry likel and also oll of my famly
and they ar oll agoing to stick by me   so you can just do just as
you feal about it   you can settle it in Kindness or in rath i can
be the nisses frend ever you had i olwas had Bin and i can again
of corse you sed you thought 8 to 10 months was ample time But it
takes money to By a home and i havent got it   i am a states man

*and have Kno town and my Boys has Bin Born and Brot up here
and it is there home   so i will Bring to a close trusting we can be
frends againe*

*But your the man to chouse it
Verry truly yours
Jim
Inclose find pitcher of Boat wolcott and i just Bilt*

In several other letters of that year to Rosy, Jim continued to request to remain on Bear Island. On June 13, 1938, he wrote:

*glad to here you are comen to island But verry sorror to here how
you feal aBout me But i have don you peapel no harm and i
think you have got the rong uner standen from last summr But
god knows oll and wolcott (Hardie) will take my place with you
until i get moved of i am Bilding a camp on scrag island   wont
Be verry good comadshens   But the Best i can do at present i have
kno money to Buy a house for my famly and i even have kno town
for i have Bin liven here on this island for 28 years and i am a
states man so now you can imeag how i feal with a Big famly but
the old saying is where theres a will theres a way so will close see
you soon truly yours Jim*

Things were still not settled by October 12, 1938, when Jim wrote Rosy to ask if the Fuller side of the family would be paying him for his work, saying that "mister King" had written Jim that he would no longer be paying Jim after June 1. Jim wrote:

*But if you feal that you dont want a careaker on Bear island i
wood like to kno and i will not stand in the way for i am not
intrest in this island life without a income you kno rossie i cant*

move wthout a cost and the fishig Bissness is gon i never got a dollar out of fishig this year and you kno i never got much out of the island But mr Dumoulin helped me a little   But it is looking pritty tuff for us this winter so i wish that if it coud be don that you and wolcott wood sqere rite up with me up to date and tell me Just what you people want me to do   if you folks want me to make eny changes in taken care of island   Juat say the word   i will not stand in the way so pleas think this matter over and settle wages up to dat and you and wolcott will look at rite side of this

In this letter Jim enclosed a newspaper clipping of poems of "Our Islands: A Series," by Capt. Walter E. Scott, including an eight-line poem titled "Bear Island."[40]

Jim's situation to continue as caretaker was clarified and resolved in a November 7, 1938, letter to him from Rosy, in which she wrote:

Dear Jim. Thank you for the clippings of the poems about Penobscot Bay, they are very nice. . . . In answer to your question about continuing as caretaker on the island, you know that I want you to continue as I have already told you last summer—my only reason for not wanting you to continue would be on account of drinking as I told you, but by keeping on doing as you did last summer there is no reason in the world why you should not keep on your job

Thus, Jim remained as caretaker, living at the Harbor House. Of note in the letters to Andy King and Rosy is that Jim repeats the phrase that he has "no town for I am a states man." This is a situation of which he was apparently quite aware, being an outsider "from away" and also not a US citizen at that time. Bear Island and the surrounding islands were located in an "unorganized township" or territory of Hancock County. As explained by John Enk in his book, cited earlier:

> Politically speaking, the resident of an unorganized township is somewhat like that of a "man without a country." There is no local government whatsoever, no local assessor, no local tax collector, no local officer for the enforcement of the law and no fire department.[41]

As a "states man," Jim's sole support and defense in the dispute over his job and his place of residence with the owners was himself and that of his family. He came out on the winning side!

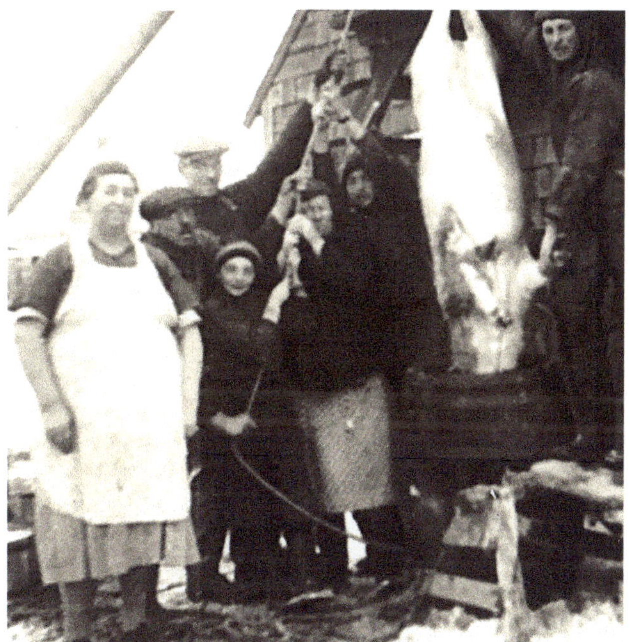

Alice and the family at the Fish House (Boat House), preparing the pig for cooking, Christmas 1941.   BEAR ISLAND FAMILY ARCHIVES

Through all of his years at Bear, his principal employer–employee relationship was with the women of the family. In general, they seemed to be more understanding with Jim than the men were.

These years of generational change of ownership and responsibility for managing the island coincided with changes within the families themselves: the lives of the young adults, their work, and their places of residence. Uneasiness about a possible sale of individual interest to outsiders added to the tension. As a result, over the next few years several heirs sold their interests to other members of the family, bowing out from their support and maintenance of the island. Andy King was one who sold his share within the family.

Following that difficult time in the late 1930s, Jim remained at Bear, living at the Harbor House, and continued as caretaker until 1945–1946. Jim and Alice had a close relationship with Rosy. She spent the entire winter of 1941–1942 on Bear, living in the cottage at one end, while the Hardies lived in the Harbor House on the other end. Jim's letters from 1943 through 1946 mention the difficulties of dealing with the winter weather and chores to be done, such as putting up the ice, which involved sawing the ice in large chunks in the pond, and then storing these in the ice house, while working alone, writing that his sons were not around to help out.

Although there are no known letters at that time between Jim and my father, there was communication. Jim's papers and application for immigration and naturalization, mentioned earlier, include a letter from my father, dated February 23, 1942. The letter is short but to the point and seems to have carried weight. It was written on letterhead from the Naval Training School of South Boston, Massachusetts, where my father was head of the Navigation School:

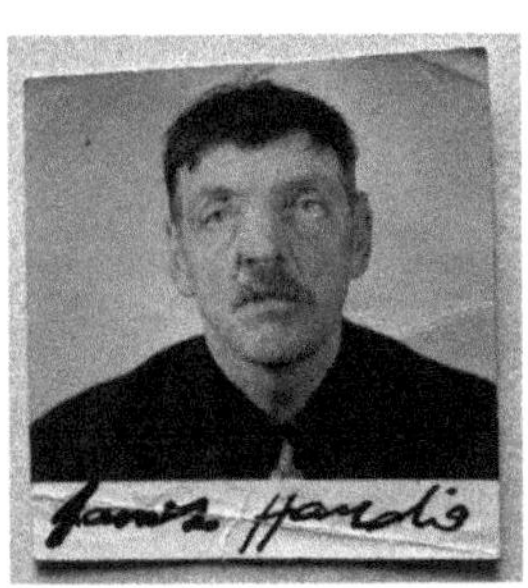

Jim's photo from his immigration and naturalization papers, 1942.
COURTESY OF
EVELYN HARDIE

Dear Captain Hardie:

This letter is to state that I have known you since 1910 and that you lived on Bear Island and have been employed by my family from time to time since that date.
I consider you to be of good character and reputation.

Yours very truly,
Wolcott Fuller, Lieut. Comdr. USNR

Wartime conditions made things harder. Food rationing was in effect, and so was gas, on which boats depended. Jim wrote to Rosy on May 27, 1943, *"But sorrow to here of not running the island But i dont see how we could for the gass questwen is offel Bad and also the food rashen it sure wood be offel hard."* Since the mid-1930s, Rosy had been taking in "paying guests" at the island as a way of making ends meet. Both family and friends were welcome, and all contributed equally for meals and linen services. During World War II, she desisted for the reasons Jim explains.

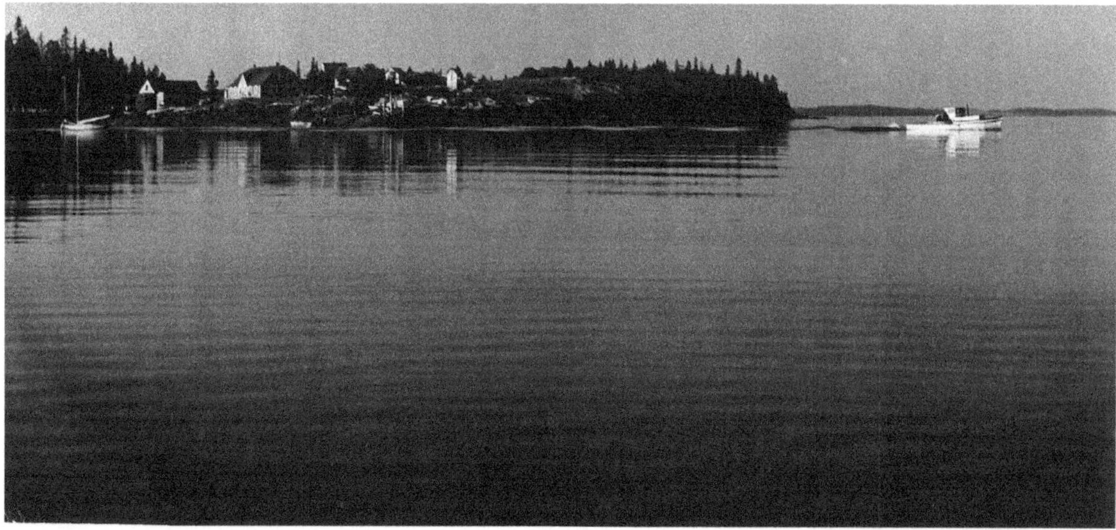

Leaving Bear Island in the morning light, heading west toward Scrag island, 1940.
GEOFFREY BAKER PHOTO

Later on, the war brought a welcome glimpse of Wolcott Fuller that Jim mentioned to Rosy, Wolcott's sister, in that same letter of May 27:

> *i see wolcott fuller a cuppel of weaks ago he came in by Scrag island in a big navey boat and i went out and see him But couldent here verry much for the engin made so much noise But it was nice to see him*

While my father was stationed at Bar Harbor on Mount Desert Island as adjunct commander of the Navy Base, he decided to bring a US Navy mine sweeper on a training mission from Bar Harbor to Bear Island. Pearl told the story that he was gathering wood on Scrag Island and was scared to see a warship coming in so close to the island, but Jim knew who it was and was quoted by Rosy as saying, "Don't worry, there's only one fool damned enough to be able to do that and it is Wolcott Fuller."

On December 25, 1943, he wrote to Rosy:

> *we are having some offel cold weather this month i hope it dont ceap up oll winter as is started   if so will Be a tuf winter o' but have to take wat comes for us   a person cant die until there time comes But one thing i dont have to worry me this winter is winslow on the water with his Boat*[42]

Jim and Alice would stay on Bear as long as they could, weather permitting, and then move into Sunset on Deer Isle for the winter months. On November 18, 1945, Jim wrote:

> *well rosey i am still on the island and will be here for some time yet i expect it will be DecemBer Befor i get away for it is such a hard Job to move a live pig and i have no one to help me handel him so i will stay late enouf and Kill him here and then i can*

handel him all rite i havent don a offel lot aBout moven yet for i
cant get any help this time of year for the wether is up and down
so and the days so short and the Boys is doing offel well lobstern
when the weathr is fit for them to get out

Jim was aware by the fall of 1945 that Rosy was looking around
for a full-time caretaker. Jim wrote in a January 22, 1946, letter:

well rosey in regards to me going Back to Bear island in march is
this way   last otom you still sead in evry letter that you wer still
planing on coming to island and you sead you cood not do eny
thing towardes geting a caretker until you came up here well i
see it got so late in season and weather Bad that there was no sho
of you geting up   we stade as late as was safe for mrs Hardie and
i to stay so i sead there woodent Be much moving around the tuf
months of the winter i wood go back in march if my helth is good
for i want to try and fix up things as usual and so as i always don
until you come up here and get another man   i will not see you
stuck for the season rosey   But rosey it is not safe for mrs Hardie
and my self to live on that island in the winter months alone so i
thought it Better for me not to Be in a good mans way

With his usual insight and instinct for survival, Jim knew the
time had come to move on. It was undoubtedly a difficult move,
and it took place slowly during 1946 while the new caretaker
learned the ropes. When weather permitted and his boat and
engine were working and he was of good health, Jim would go to
Bear and stay out at the camp at Piggie's Point. Winslow was working at Great Spruce Head, and Wolcott was fishing around the
island. The Hardie presence shifted its venue but remained in the
Bay, as they do to this day.

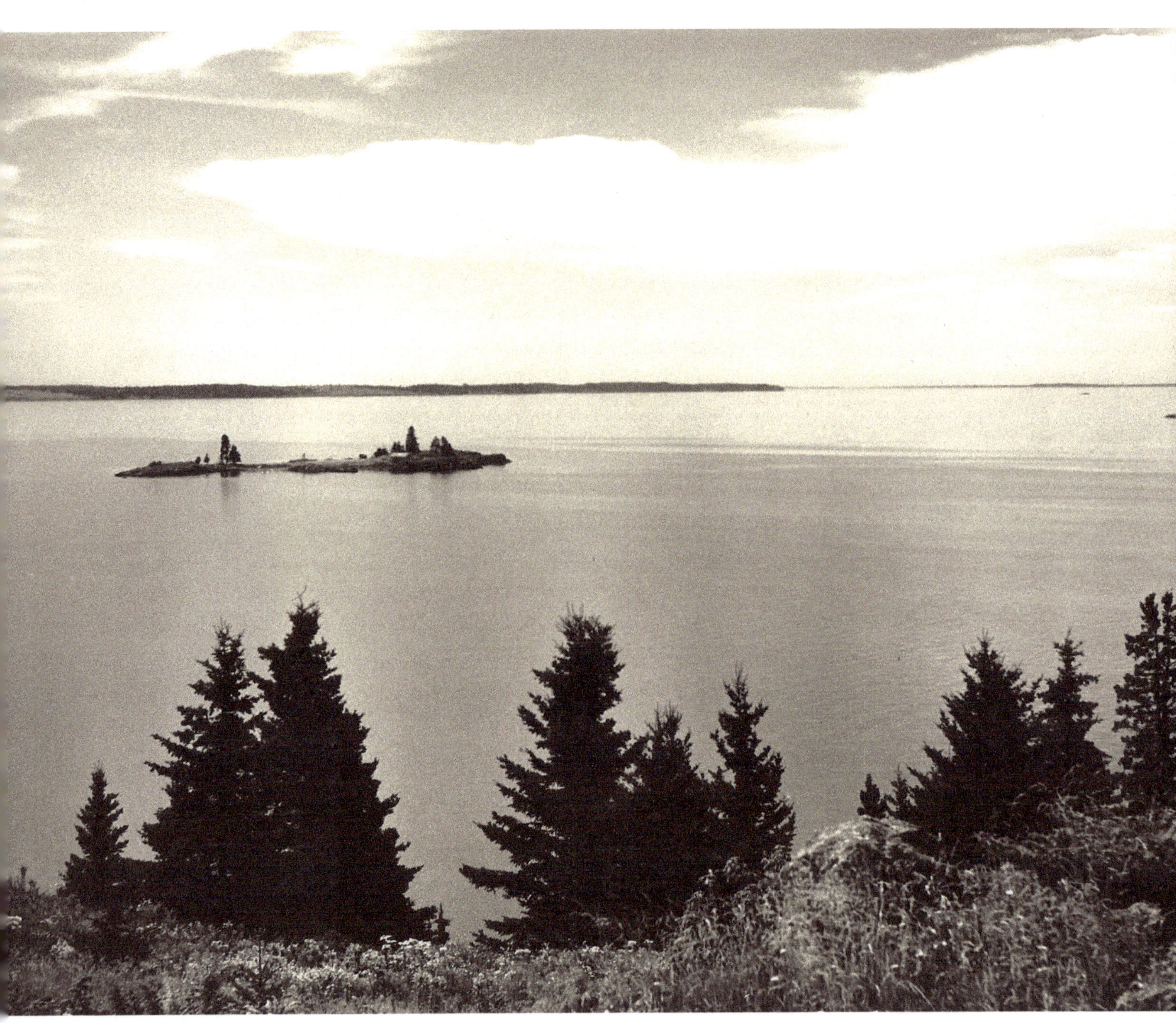

View from Great Spruce Head Island of Scrag Island, with North Haven in the background, 1940.
GEOFFREY BAKER PHOTO

Scrag Island and Passing On

After Jim was no longer formally connected with Bear in an employee–employer situation, Scrag Island became his island foothold in Penobscot Bay. With uncanny foresight, he had purchased Scrag Island from the Eaton Family as early as 1930. Jim used Scrag, about a quarter of a mile from Bear, for tending his weirs and keeping sheep. He built a rustic camp there for overnight stays.

By 1946, he deemed it would have to be comfortable enough for him and Alice to move there. The Harbor House on Bear was no longer their home. Jim and Alice continued to live on Scrag during the spring, summer, and fall, as long as it was seasonally possible, just as they had done on Bear. They spent the winters in Sunset on Deer Isle in a their house. Jim continued to fish for a living. As on Bear Island, Jim and Alice were the only full-time residents of Scrag Island, a five-acre island according to the deed.

By the 1950s, Jim knew his health was failing. He made the decision to sell Scrag to his son Wolcott, who was a full-time fisherman in Penobscot Bay. This he did six months before he died. Jim and Alice were witnesses of the deed of that sale, dated April 5, 1954. In that way, Jim, with his lifelong sense of survival and

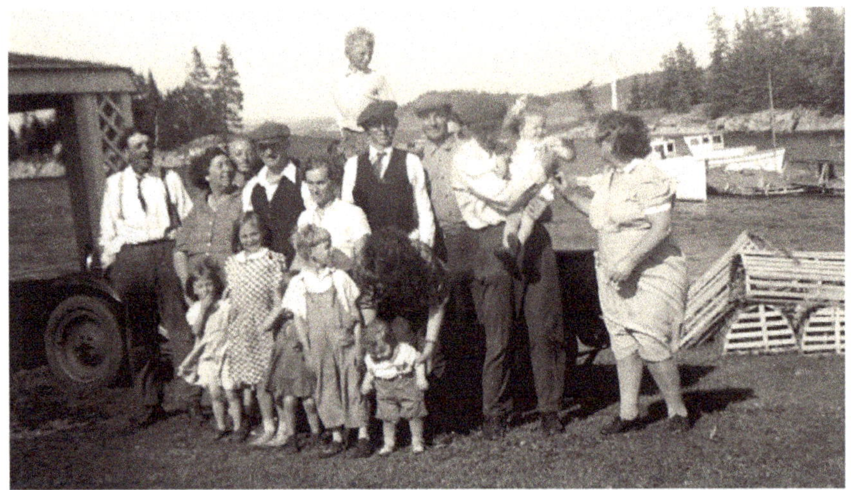

Gathering of three generations of Hardies at the Harbor House, 1944.
BEAR ISLAND FAMILY ARCHIVES

looking out for himself and his family, ensured that Scrag Island would remain in the family.

Pearl told me that in August of 1954 Jim suffered a heart attack while they were dealing with their boats and the aftermath of a hurricane, and that, shortly after, he suffered another heart attack while sawing wood in the yard on Scrag. Hurricanes Carol and Edna were deadly storms that wreaked havoc on all of the islands from August 31 to September 11 that year. On October 8, 1954, a few days after his seventieth birthday, Jim collapsed and died of a last heart attack, at the water's edge on the shore of Scrag, while cutting up alders for his weir.

After a hiatus, my father's collection of letters had resumed in 1953. The next to last letter from Jim in my father's collection is dated February 9, 1953, mailed from the Sunset post office. Jim had learned that my parents were looking for a house to buy in Sunset on Deer Isle, where Jim and Alice lived in the winters. He wrote:

*in hopes of going Back to the island in erlye spring so hopen you
and famly can get down some weak end while you are here you
and famly can stay with us i have plenty room so you wont have
to worry i here you was looking for a house it is a hard joB to doo
Bissnes like that in such a short time so it maB so you could use
my house this summer and give you a chance to look around wich
i will be over on island durn summer i Be glad to help you so and
to hav your famly get down to maine in the summer wich i know
mrs fuller is so scared of the water But Wolcott if you get her close
as sunset she may get a Jump across some time*

The last letter from Jim to my father is written on April 24, 1954:
*frend Wolcott Just a line in regards to the 2 houses down the reach
which we went and lookd at i wend over to see the town manger
and he sed there wasant much hopes of them places at present he
sead that it is ear [heir] ship property and they wont agrea with
each other and there is about 20 aKers of land to each one so he
sed if he can do eny thing he wood get in tuch with you By me so
will close from Jim*

Indeed, my mother was not fond of being "on the water." She
and my father did buy, sight unseen, a fully furnished, winterized
house in Sunset in 1954, the year Jim died. Day trips to Bear from
Sunset during the summer allowed my father to continue to spend
some time on Bear Island until he too passed away in 1959.

Wolcott Hardie subsequently sold Scrag Island to Montgomery Hare in 1960. Rob Hare, Montgomery's son, told a story of
one evening in the late 1960s, while he was spending the night with
Alice Hardie, Pearl, and Evelyn in Sunset, when Alice, out of the
blue, recounted Jim's last day on Scrag. She said Jim knew he was

not well and had an intuition that his time had come. She said he knew this because he asked Alice as a special request to make him an apple pie. It was while she was making an apple pie that he died at the water's edge.

Mrs. Hardie's strength to deal with and survive a wide range of situations, from birth to death, from a life lived on an island is revealed in a remembrance told by her younger sister, Abby Shepard Weed, in an interview in 1975.[43] Abby related that her brother-in-law, Jim Hardie, "dropped dead on the shore." Her sister Alice "heisted a white sheet on a flagpole" as a signal to Pearl, who was out lobstering in the Bay. According to Abby, Pearl knew what the raised white sheet meant. He went straight to Great Spruce Head Island to get his brother Wolcott, who was caretaking there. The two of them went directly to Stonington on Deer Isle to get the undertaker, and then they went to Scrag Island.

One of the most touching letters in my father's collection is the last one. It is from Alice, dated December 29, 1954, after Jim died. Alice writes:

> *i miss Jim a lot for I fill I have lost the best frend I had and a few days befor Jim did He ask perl woud He take care of me if He past out and perl say yes He word so we are in Sunset now and if you come this way plese come in and see me and pearl and wife so good luck to all*

Jim and Alice were married for 45 years. After he died, Alice lived in Sunset on Deer Isle, with her youngest son, Pearl, and his wife, Evelyn, and their four children, until she passed away in 1975. Jim and Alice are buried side by side in the Hillside Cemetery of Deer Isle, Maine.

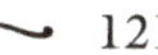

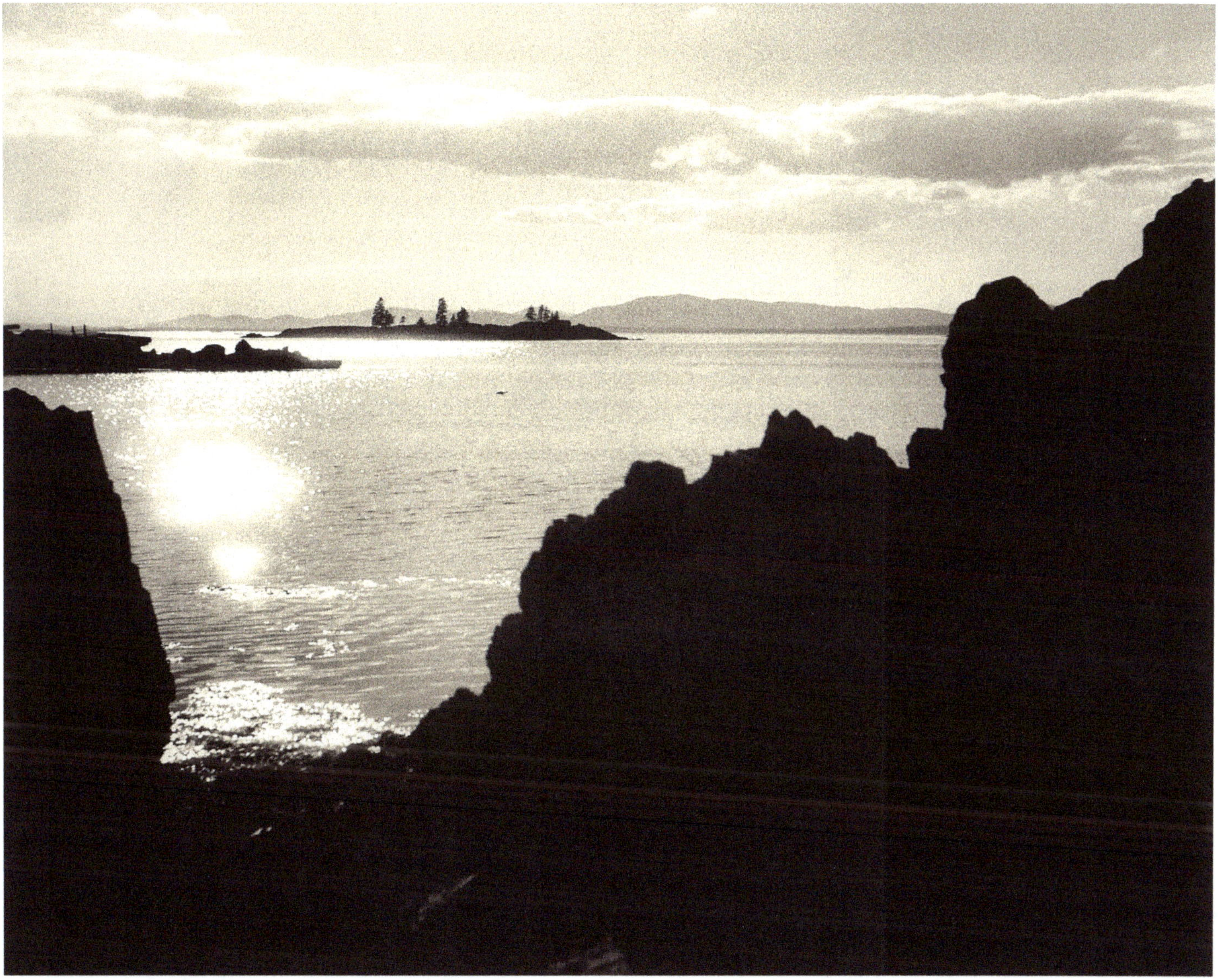

Scrag Island, with Camden Hills in the background, from Camp Point (Piggie's Point), 1940. GEOFFREY BAKER PHOTO

Jim and Alice's descendants continue to live and work in Penobscot Bay. Pearl C. Hardie, their youngest son, was a fisherman and lobsterman as well as the caretaker on Bear Island from 1955 until 1973. During the summers, he; his wife, Evelyn; and their four children, Barbara, Christine, Pearl K., and Phyllis, lived at the Harbor House. To this day they refer to the Harbor House as home. Pearl Senior, as we called him, passed away in Deer Isle in 2011. Pearl K. is a full-time fisherman and lobsterman. He and his family live year-round on Deer Isle, and they like to spend a weekend at the Harbor House in the fall.

Wolcott Hardie fished and lobstered in the Bay throughout his life and was caretaker of Great Spruce Head from October 1951 until October 1955. Wolcott Hardie died in 1993 in Deer Isle. His son Reynold was the caretaker on Great Spruce Head from 1969 until 1983, living year-round on the island, and now lives on Deer Isle.

Some of Jim's great-grandchildren and other Hardie relatives living on Deer Isle and environs choose to continue to make a living from the sea. They do so under greatly changed conditions from those of a century ago. Yesterday's fishermen are today's and tomorrow's marine aquaculture fishers or fishing people, working with global sea life and climate changes, meeting the demands of the seasons and nature. They do so with Jim's same love of the sea and a spirit of dedication to a way of life of independence, self–reliance, and endurance.

Letters

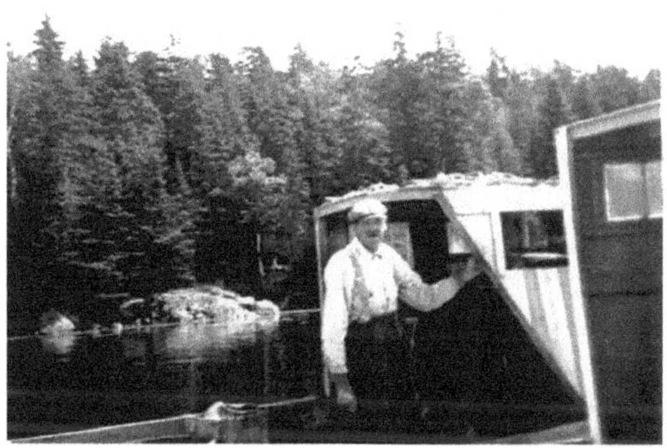

Jim in his boat at the dock at Bear Island, 1953. PERSIS CAROLINE FULLER ALDEN PHOTO

November 14, 1915

Jones, Hardie

Dear frend wilket i was set don to drop you a few lins in anser to your letter there is was offel glad to here from you well wilket you asked me if i got the boat the ol site indied that i tel you wilket you foaks you got away from the island in time for we had a terrebel big storm and after the storm was over the wind come north and it blode a livin geal well wilket i sopes you herd about the in of dark harber burnen down it burnt down the same week you left it made a brote fire for a little wile it was just 2 ours from the time the fire started and it was all burnt flat to the ground well wilket

Three-page letter from Jim Hardie to Wolcott Fuller, November 14, 1915— page 1.

i have not started scloper
yet but i am agoin to start
next week well wilket i thank
you for sending the childrens pictys
i think they look verry common
well wilket dit you here that
my James come verry nere geten
klot i will tell you just hou it
hapend we was up to little Dear island
one sunday and we was comen hone in the
earlen and James went to blact in
the caben and we was oll out in
the cockpit we got down to the end
of chainlinks and we herd a noise
in the caben and there was the
pore little feller streched out
on the caben flore where he had fell
agast the knot engens fly weal
and it struck him over the rite
ie and it gave him a nofel cut
so i turned my Boat and put
to the Doctors and he hade to have
4 stiches put in it and i cood not
put him — a sleep so he had to suffer

Three-page letter from Jim Hardie to Wolcott Fuller, November 14, 1915—continued, page 2.

536

oll the pain But he is oll
well now and is smart
and we are oll well at present
and hopen those fou lines will
find you the same well eavery
thing is oll rite at the island
from James Hardie
eazel postofice
Deor island
Maine
to frend wolcot
fuller

**Three-page letter from Jim Hardie to Wolcott Fuller, November 14, 1915—
continued, page 3.**

January the 3, 1917

Dear friend wolcot
i now drop you a few lines
in anser to your letter
well wolcot i was verry
glad to here from you
and to here that you are
well and geting along good
at your scool we are oll
well at present But the
Baby was verry sick
last weak But he is
petter now well wolcot
yet i have not received
the hat that you sent
me yet i have bin looking
for it every mail day
But have not got it yet
so i thought i wood
let you no about it

Three-page letter from Jim Hardie to Wolcott Fuller, January 3, 1917—page 1.

2
well wolcott we have
had some offel bad weather
this winter so far it is
a snowstorm to night i
was over to canden yestday
i had quite a kreak coming
home it is hard to get
a chance to get of the
island it blous a
gal of wind every day
well wolcot we are laten
in our new part on the
house now and we are very
comfbol now i ciled my
pig December 27 and
December 28 i ciled my
black calf and i
wish you could of bin
here to help me well
every thing is all rite
on the island well
yo say you are sending

ne the paper and i
thank you verry much
i think it is offel good of
you i hope i shall be
abel to do as much for
you some time well
wolcott i ame sending
you the pitcher of the
wigo when i holeld
her up you will see
my crue posing with
me on the pakel
and the other part
of my crue on the end
of the wauf so i will
bring this to a close for
this time hoper to here
from you soon agai
yours truely
from James Hardie
eagel mair

Three-page letter from Jim Hardie to Wolcott Fuller, January 3, 1917, mentioning everyone has influenza— continued, pages 2 and 3.

Jan 12 / 1919
Bear island
aline

Dear frend wilcot in anser to yours of november 30/1918 in wich i was very glad to here from you wich i see that you are a long ways from home well wolcot glad to here you say that you will Be to the island next summer for you seam to Be the main stay here at the island in the summer well wolcot the negouisefiro last summer after you left we got good sirvice of her well wolcot i Kiled my ugly Bull

a week ago and he was offel ugly when i got him of litle spruce well wolcot every thing is just the same as when you left But we have had a prettie Bad fall for we oll had the inflinza and had it hard and you remember her[illegible] he Died with it But we are oll well now hopen this find you the same So i will Bring this to a close for this tim eken yours Jamy Hardie eagel post ofice Bear island aline

Two-page letter from Jim Hardie to Wolcott Fuller, January 3, 1917—pages 1 and 2.

February 9 1934

To James Hardie
Eagle

Dear frend wolcott your letter received monday & was very glad to her from you and to her you are well But very sorrow and suprised to her of your mother death i sure will mice her she has bin a verry good frend to me well wolcott this sure is a tuff winter her the Bay is frosen up our boats frose in the harbor we can walk to little spruse and to narf island down. to we X too hed and crab tree a point worth drive i am giting those few lines but dont no when i will get to the post ofice wether offel cold Stern ther 12 Belo zero this morning it frost up ice last weak had 20 inch thick there is nothing we can do now but put it loost isten our Boats and cut wood for stoves wolcott and i was over to spruce head and helped to post the ice up over there 2 weeks ago only had 12 inches we are agoing to a post up orother cutting next week we are all well at island that winter to be thankful for this offel winter wolcott goes gunning once and a wile to hass tive away he got 2 wisslers yestday and he got 2 to hav we ar agoing to hav they backed for dinner Sunday dear frend Jisse gitta few lines more this feB 11 havent got to post ofice yet and donte no how long it will be before i get there there is so much ice it isent safe to walk and cant get a boat out well wolcott i was over to great spruce head today putting the second cuttin of ice and send Howard hote the mail there to us today so i recived your letter of feBuary 5 and check for jenuary and tharkley am verry much for the exonshe

Two-page letter from Jim Hardie to Wolcott Fuller, February 9, 1934, written on three different days—page 1.

your mother hant payed me up for December i will inclose the last letter i received from her so as there will be no miss under standing well Wolcott the ice breaker boat name de Kickabue is having quit a job Braking ice in penoscott Bay this winter she is coming to eagel island tomorow with some supplies she has Bin to north haven and stonton and to swans island and she is clearing the usstern chanel from Between isboro and little space for the Big trank steamers to get there to stocton springs corner either or ill dont no of eny thing now for present time so will call to a close for now

February 16 still ice Bound But Bones war got to spring bed last night and its going to eagel today and i am agoing to try and give him this litter to maly so will close
Best regards from all to all
James Hardie
eagel
maine

Two-page letter from Jim Hardie to Wolcott Fuller, February 9, 1934—continued, page 2.

May 10 1937

Dear frend wolcott Just a few lines to let you Kno how thigs is going at ishard well going fine had verry plesit winter But lots of rain not not so good for winter wether had a verry coold Back uord spring But geting verry good now But ground verry wet we are all well at ishard except my self and i am having offel hard luck now now i will tell you march 31 rite in the Best of my s eloping i was close tow the Bank prying logs with a croBar to get it up so as i could saw it for wood and my Bar sliped and i fell over the Bank in a rock pile But got out of it with Just a sprant ankel But that laid me up for 2 weaks for i weak i couldent

Three-page letter from Jim Hardie to Wolcott Fuller, May 10, 1937—page 1.

poot my 2 foot to the floor
well i pest got so i could
work good so last friday
march 7 i went over to dunbar
to bring the children home
for weak end and i went
to step from the warf on to
my boat and my foot sliped
and fell agenst my hores
hurting my side so i brot my
famly home and i got home
i couldent set down or lay
down so next morning the
boys toof me to casten
to the doctor he put me three
ex ray and found i had
broke a rik so he plastered
me up and told me not to do
a thing for 3 weaks and i
have to see him again in a
few days but it is a offel
thing for me to lay up for 3 weak
but the way i feal i am glad
to well wolcott i had a
letter from mr king

saying he wood be coming
down to the island for sumer
and he send he wood rite
you in regards to boats
so i rot him telling him there
is kno enging in wego i
sold the enging that was
in her for $300 so i think
it wood be rite for them to
poot one in the wego if you
let them have the boat but
i havent herd from him in
regards yet about it well
hoper it will be so as you
and famly can get down
to island sumtine dern
summer so will bring to
close for this and i get out
to work again i am in
bed riting this letter
verry truely yours
James Hardie
eagel
m a e

Three-page letter from Jim Hardie to Wolcott Fuller, May 10, 1937—continued, pages 2 and 3.

MR. JAMES HARDIE
BEAR ISLAND
SUNSET P. O., MAINE

febuary 9 1953

friend. Wolcott just a few lines in answer and thanks to you for the rembers of armt to me i herd of you Being down to sunset last fall sorrow i couldent of Knowing and got over and see ya But hope you get down again will i am living here now living in sunset for the winter and in hopes of going back to the island erlye spring so hopen you and famly can get down some deaf end while we are here you and famly can stay with us i have pienty room so you wont haye to worry i here you was looking for a house it is a hard of Job to doo Bisaness like that in a such a short time so it mab so you could use my house this summer and give you a chance to look around which i will be over on island dirrin summer i Be glad

Two-page letter from Jim Hardie to Wolcott Fuller, February 9, 1953, the next to last letter from Jim—page 1.

To help you so as to hav your famley
get down to Maine in the summer
wich i kno mrs Fuller is to scared
of the watter But Wolcott if you get her
as close as sunset she may get a jump
across. Some tim will Wolcott having
verry modret winter So far and
we ar oll well at present an hope this
find you and famly the same So will
close for this time

Best regards.
To you and famly
from Jim

**Two-page letter from Jim Hardie to Wolcott Fuller, February 9, 1953,
the next to last letter from Jim—continued, page 2.**

Acknowledgments

Over the years so many have helped me tell the Jim Hardie story, reading and rereading pieces and offering ideas and suggestions. My husband, Tom Marvel, encouraged me in this endeavor until he passed away in 2015; this included accompanying me on our trip to experience Prince Edward Island firsthand. When, in March 2020, the COVID 19 pandemic hit and we were asked to shelter in place, there awaited Jim's letters, folders of gathered material, and ample time to at last focus fully on his saga.

I'm ever grateful to the Hardie family for sharing their anecdotes and memories, as acknowledged in the Preface. Especially wonderful were talks with Pearl C. Hardie, Jim's youngest son, now deceased; and his wife, Evelyn. Their oldest daughter, Barbara Hardie Bray, recently told me that she welcomed this opportunity to learn more about her grandfather, who died before she was born. Her siblings, Christine Hardie Ebert, Pearl K. Hardie, and Phyllis Hardie, all read the manuscript, as did Reynold Hardie, their cousin, who is Wolcott Hardie's son.

The support and interest from Tom Marvel, my youngest son, has been fundamental to my decision to go ahead with this book, and he responded, "It's a go" upon reading the first draft with photos. Elena Lawton de Torruella and Margo Miller, writers themselves, have been my constant, in-house editors, along with Rachel Brown, Jessica Lipnack, and Molly Batchelder. Family members who have read the drafts, contributed suggestions, and borne with good humor hearing about it over the years are Deacon Marvel, my oldest son; Jonathan Marvel, my middle son; and Elsa Marvel, Daphne Marvel, Xavier Marvel, Pablo Marvel, Diego Marvel, Solal Marvel, Marie-Laure Grimaldi-Marvel, Persis Caroline Fuller Alden, Jo Marvel Hull, and Professor of History Emeritus Dr. Richard Hull. Thanks also to my year-round, on-the-ground Maine family, Andy and Abby Fuller, Alexandra Snyder May, Sam May, and Kariska K. Puchalski, keen and helpful contributors all. Sincere thanks as well to Lourdes Miranda, Carmen Dolores Hernandez, Michelle Sugden, Pat Molther Rosenberg, Sarah Faragher, and Rob Hare for their careful and sensitive reading.

Millie Rahn provided useful editing services. Jill Pellarin was the excellent copy editor and final proofreader, along with Abby Fuller, and I remain highly appreciative of their contributions. My gratitude to Lindy Gifford of Manifest Identity for her professional publishing guidance, book design work, and patience, ever present throughout the process of making the book a reality. Thanks to Isabel Jane Marvel for creating the four maps for this book that illustrate Jim's lifetime voyage from Scotland to Scrag Island. I am fortunate that Anne Baker White, a photographer herself, provided permission to use the stunning photographs taken in 1940 by her father, Geoffrey Baker. A special thanks to Philip Conkling for writing the Forward. Founder of the Island Institute and president from 1983 until 2013, his formidable knowledge of Maine coastal island life and its inhabitants lends Jim Hardie the remarkable context he deserves.

Notes

1   R. Buckminster Fuller, "The Bear Island Story," in *Bear Island Centennial Book 1904–2004*, ed., Lucilla Fuller Marvel (San Juan, Puerto Rico: Doubledey, 2009), 25. The story was originally written in 1967.

2   Lucilla Fuller Marvel, "The Hardie Family," in *Bear Island Centennial Book, 1904–2004*, ed., Lucilla Fuller Marvel (San Juan, Puerto Rico: Doubledey, 2009), 73–87.

3   Lucilla Fuller Marvel, "The Life and Letters of Jim Hardie: Fisherman, Farmer, Captain, Caretaker," *Island Journal* 28 (2012), 66–70.

4   Barbara Bray Hardie, Jim's granddaughter and oldest daughter of Pearl and Evelyn Hardie, visited Scotland with her husband, Jim Bray, in 2002, to learn more about her grandfather's origins. She found two people by the name of James Hardie listed in the General Register Office of Edinburgh, Scotland for 1884: one on October 12 and one on October 22.

5   Dawn Hopkins, "Home Children on Prince Edward Island," *Island Magazine* 65 (2009): 26.

6   Kenneth Bagnell, *The Little Immigrants: The Orphans Who Came to Canada* (Toronto: The DunDurn Group, 2001).

7   Bagnell, 35.

8   Bagnell, 29.

9   "About: Background." *British Home Children Special Interest Group*, https://bhc.ogs.on.ca/about/.

10   Bagnell, 206.

11   Hopkins, "Home Children," 27. See also Sara Underwood, *Awful Kind: The Story of the Middlemore Children of Prince Edward Island* (Amazon Kindle, 2018), which documents the lives of many of the children sent from Scotland to Liverpool, to Halifax, and then settled in individual homes.

12   Hopkins, "Home Children," 26.

13   Evelyn Hardie, interview by Lucilla F. Marvel, June 23, 2013, Sunset, Maine.

14   The American William Dane Phelps published his memoirs of decades of life at sea, including working on sealers in Antarctica, in his 1871 journal *Fore and Aft; Or, Leaves from the Life of an Old Sailor* (Whitefish, Montana: Kessinger, 2010).

15   According to Charles B. McLane and Caroline Everts McLane, *Islands of the Mid-Maine Coast: Vol. 1, Penobscot Bay*, rev. ed. (Woolwich, ME: The Kennebec River Press, 1997), 255.

16   Fuller, "Bear Island Story," 24.

17   Fuller, 24.

18   Letter of Rosamond Fuller Kenison to Susan Alden, granddaughter of Wolcott Fuller, May 16, 1971, reproduced in the *Bear Island Centennial Book 1904–2004*, 31.

19   McLane and McLane, *Islands of the Mid-Maine Coast*, 257.

20   According to the 1904 deed, Bear contained "forty-two acres more or less." Later documents refer to forty-four acres.

21   Kenison, letter to Susan Alden, 33.

22   "A History of Great Spruce Head Island," prepared in 2013, covering many stories of the Porters' one hundred years of ownership and enjoyment, contains a list of caretakers on Great Spruce Head Island from 1913 until 2013, and on Bear Island from 1948 to 1955. It is an unpublished document.

23   McLane and McLane, *Islands of the Mid-Maine Coast*, 248.

24 Abby Shepard Weed, recorded interview by Lisa Schneider, July 2, 1975, part of a series of oral history recording by the Maine Folklife Center MF 048, a project of the University of Maine Anthropology Department, NA0995.

25 Wolcott E. Hardie, recorded interview by James Bannon, July 17, 1975, part of a series of oral history recording by the Maine Folklife Series MF 048, a project of the University of Maine Anthropology Department, NA0993.

26 Wolcott E. Hardie interview.

27 John C. Enk, *A Family Island in Penobscot Bay: The Story of Eagle Island, based Largely on the Recollections of Captain Erland L. Quinn* (Rockland, ME: Courier-Gazette, 1973), p. 96.

28 Winslow Hardie, recorded interview by Kariska Puchalski and Andrew Russo, Deer Isle, Maine, March 2004.

29 Wolcott E. Hardie interview.

30 Fuller, "Bear Island Story," 25.

31 Kenison, letter to Susan Alden, 33.

32 It could have been the *Boston Daily Post* or the *Boston Herald*.

33 Fuller, "Bear Island Story," 33.

34 Kenison, letter to Susan Alden, 33.

35 McLane and McLane, *Islands of the Mid-Maine Coast*, 250. The Enk book on Eagle Island also mentions these "recycling" activities on Eagle and Bear.

36 Wolcott E. Hardie interview.

37 Kariska Puchalski recalls that Rosy Fuller Kenison, her mother, often recounted this incident. Marjorie DuMoulin, Lucy's daughter, visited Bear Island in September 2004 and corroborated the incident. She accompanied her mother's remains to Chicago.

38 "Fisherman near Death as Gas Tanks Explode." Tuesday April 29, 1943. A newspaper clipping of this article was sent by Jim to Rosy with his May 27, 1943, letter. (The clipping does not include the banner or page numbers.)

39 Winslow Hardie interview.

40 Captain Walter E. Scott, "Bear Island," in *Poems of Coastal New England, 1941* (New York, NY: Beacon).

41 Enk, *A Family Island*, 207–208.

42 Winslow Hardie survived a serious boating accident in 1938 and no longer had his own boat.

43 Abby Shepard Weed interview.

About the Author

Lucilla Fuller Marvel, born and educated in Massachusetts, moved in 1959 to the island of Puerto Rico with her husband, Thomas S. Marvel, and three-month-old son. She has lived ever since in San Juan, Puerto Rico's capital, raising two more sons, practicing social and urban planning, and enjoying seven grandchildren. Her teaching and BA in architectural sciences from Harvard College and MP in planning from the University of Puerto Rico have led to several books, including *Listen to What They Say: Planning and Community Development in Puerto Rico*, published by the Editorial Press of the University of Puerto Rico, 2008; and *Planificación para un Puerto Rico Sostenible: Fundamentos del Proceso*, coauthored with L. Cuadrado Pitterson, M. Maldonado LaFontaine, E. Moreno Ortiz, and M. Villariny Marrero, and published by Ediciones Puerto, 2016.

The other island in her life is Bear Island, in Penobscot Bay, Maine, where she has known the Hardie family all of her life, including Jim Hardie, during her time spent there in summers. The two islands share similar longitudes (San Juan, Puerto Rico, 66.16 W; Bear Island, Maine, 68.49 W) but contrasting latitudes (San Juan, 18.47 N; Bear Island, 44.22 N), and they both share territorial status. Puerto Rico is an unincorporated territory of the United States of America, and Bear Island is in an unorganized territory in Hancock County, Maine.

www.ingramcontent.com/pod-product-compliance
Lightning Source LLC
Chambersburg PA
CBHW040207110726
48005CB00019B/2933